My Third Parents

My Third Parents
Orphanage to an American Dream

Fernando Kuehnel

Second Edition
© 2015 by Fernando Kuehnel. All rights reserved.

No part of this publication may be reproduced, stored in a retrieval system, or transmitted in any form or by any means—electronic, mechanical, photocopying, recording, scanning, or otherwise—except under the terms of the Copyright, Designs, and Patents Act of 1988 or under the terms of a license issued by the Copyright Licensing Agency Ltd.

ISBN: 1490449132
ISBN 13: 9781490449135

Legal Disclaimer

The publisher and the author make no representations or warranties with respect to the accuracy or completeness of the contents of this work and specifically disclaim all warranties, including without limitation warranties of fitness for a particular purpose. No warranty may be created or extended by sales or promotional materials. The advice and strategies contained herein may not be suitable for every situation.

Neither the publisher nor the author shall be liable for damages arising herefrom. The fact that an organization or website is referred to in this work as a citation and/or a potential source of further information does not mean that the author or the publisher endorses the information the organization or website may provide or recommendations it may make.

Further, readers should be aware that Internet websites listed in this work may have changed or disappeared between the time when this work was written and when it is read.

This book is dedicated to
my brothers, Adriano and Roberto Kuehnel;
my parents, Reno and Rebecca Kuehnel;
and adoptees and their parents.

Reno (Skip) & Rebecca (Becky) Kuehnel

Acknowledgments

It took ten years to write this book. It was a decade of agonizing indecision to release my feelings publically. Each time I reviewed my writing, it brought back memories I often wanted to bury into the abyss. It was my mother, Rebecca Kuehnel, who encouraged me to put my feelings on paper—probably to admonish me from not acting them out. My sister, Jean Kuehnel, pushed me to "just write it down" and not to worry about the syntax. A professor at Winona State University pushed me to keep writing and sent me to the writing center to improve my English.

I want to thank Annie Kuehnel, the mother of my two boys Fernado Jr. and Tyler. Without my kids, I would not have been able to know how a child should be loved by their parents. The moment they were born, I was able to imagine how my biological parents could have felt. When my children were born, my love was immediate and undescribable. My children also taught me how difficult parenting could be. I am forever grateful for all parents—foster parents and adoptive parents—who have taken children outside their biological circle to provide them with love and life.

Contents

	Prologue	xv
Part I	The Philippines	1
1	Abandoned	3
2	Somewhere Far Away From Home	7
3	Nayon Ng Kabataan	30
4	The Streets	60
5	The Farm	83
6	A New Beginning	95
Part II	America	101
7	The Mays	103
8	The Kuehnels	136
9	College, Camp, and Love	156
	Epilogue	189
	About the Author	199

Prologue

I remember standing at the edge of a river, my thin fingers gripping the cold railing that ran alongside the bridge. My bony arms and sunken face were black from the night's filthy work. My shirt, which barely covered my swollen stomach, had fresh stains. A banana peel hung from the pocket of my tattered shorts as I held a pineapple rind. My knees were covered with infected sores. The soles of my bare feet were covered in blistering cracks from walking on the hot asphalt chasing my next meal.

I closed my eyes as the moon rose higher over the sleeping city, illuminating the drifting mass of tin cans, plastic bottles, and torn shopping bags floating along the dark river. Confusion tangled my young mind; my life resembled the polluted river below. I felt a tear roll down my cheek as I compared life back in the orphanage with this life on the streets and realized that I was not better off in either situation.

I lowered my chin to my chest and silently mouthed a prayer: "Dear Jesus, do you know where my mommy is? Please help me find her, and please take care of my brothers while I'm gone."

My lips stopped moving as I breathed heavily, eyes closed. Crippling loneliness and desperation pierced my heart, bursting forth in a river of tears as my spirit heaved in cries of self-pity and despair.

These feelings of despair haunted me for most of my life; they were a source of many secret tears I struggled with well into my adulthood. I spent many hours trying to find the missing puzzle piece within me. It was difficult because I did not know how to put the puzzle together, and I was not sure exactly which piece was missing. Most of the time, when people feel lonely, they know the reason. Somebody died or someone stole the heart of their lover. But I would feel lonely and not know why. I would feel alone even when I was surrounded by friends and family. It is this kind engineering of the soul and mind that is difficult to solve. Yet it is also fuels my strength to overcome the darkness I felt.

I did overcome this darkness, but I did not do it alone. I am writing this book to tell you about my life, my struggle, my success, and those people who helped me through it.

I lived with numerous "parents," and I am thankful for their love. Any parents who take in children other than their biological children are special people. My third parents are incredible people whose sacrifice I can never match. I know because I have three children of my own.

I want to tell you my story…my story of growing in an orphanage, living on the streets of Manila, and finally finding my true mom and dad.

Part 1
The Philippines

Chapter 1

Abandoned

"Mama! Where are you?! Where did you go? Mama, Mama!?"

All three of us cried loudly and desperately. I was the loudest. I was the eldest of the three—two years older than Adriano, who was four years old at that time, and four years older than Bobby, who was two. I was scared. We were in the crowded, wet market where my mother had taken us to go get some food. The market was full of people shopping for vegetables and fish. We were standing in the path of heavy human traffic as people swarmed by us from all directions.

As I looked ahead, all I could see were knees and feet. I looked up and shouted, "Mama, Mama!" Adriano and Bobby started crying; I guess they sensed the fear in my voice as I called for my mother. I told Adriano to hold Bobby's hand tight, and I encircled them without letting them out of my sight. I shouted again, "Mama! Mama! Where are you?" I pivoted my body full circle, looking up at the adults passing me with the hope that I would see my mother's face or she would hear me and see me. Everyone else looked down at me, hearing my call, but they kept walking by.

We were in Quezon City, in the Project 8 district. Quezon City is the second largest city in the Philippines and was the capital then (April 15, 1974). We cried and screamed for our mother as we wandered lost through the streets. "Where are you, Mama, Mama!"

Old jeeps and rickshaws rattled past, and sellers beckoned to passers-by as shoppers bargained and haggled. Stray dogs sniffed for food in the gutters.

"Mama!"

People moved in and out in swarms, but somehow no one noticed us three little boys, terrified, anxious, and desperate. My brothers were clinging on either side of me. Our father had left us after a fight my parents had had months earlier; now our mother had vanished. The only clear memory I have today is of my dad leaving late one night when I heard them fighting. I remember my mother watching my dad walk away, disappearing into the dead of the night. We all were standing outside our house: Bobby, Adriano, my mom, and me. She was holding Bobby in her arms.

"Mama, come get us! Mama, we're over here!"

We kept crying and calling for our mother, shouting for her over and over through the crowd. We wandered the streets of Project 8 for hours, disoriented, petrified, and overwhelmed by the scary, unfamiliar world around us. No one answered our calls, and it felt like hours had turned into days.

"Mom, where are you?"

Wherever I looked, faces swarmed past—faces I did not recognize, disinterested faces that barely glanced in our direction. I was frantic. Bobby, only a toddler at that time, did not know what was going on, but he was in hysterics because his older brothers were screaming and crying for help.

"*Mommy…!*"

We wandered the streets in tears until we lost track of time, overwhelmed by fear and confusion. I felt like it was my duty to keep my brothers safe and to find my mom or my house, but I was so overwhelmed by fear that I did not know what to do. *What should I do? Where should I turn for help?* My mother was nowhere to be found. My heart was racing; my head was turning left and right, scanning frantically for a clue. As our desperation grew into a helpless panic, a sympathetic face emerged from the crowd.

A young, simply dressed woman with long, black hair and a kind smile, probably a mother herself judging by the concerned look on her face, knelt in front of me as the tears ran down my cheeks, and she looked at Bobby.

"It is OK. I am Jovita." She asked my little brother, "What's your name?"

"That's Bobby," I said as he hiccupped through tears. I wiped my tears with the bottom of my T-shirt.

"What's wrong?" She was looking at me and then asked me, "Where is your mother?"

I shrugged my shoulders and said, "Mama got lost."

"We can't find her," Adriano added with certainty.

"Can you find my mother for us?" I asked, staring at her pleadingly.

"I will help you," she said. "Don't worry. We'll find your mom." It was a relief when I heard those words.

"She will find Mama," I told my brothers.

She held Bobby's small hand as she knocked on doors and spoke to strangers. "Do you know these boys?" Jovita asked everyone we came across.

"Do you know these kids?" she asked when a woman opened the door. The woman glanced at us and shook her head before shutting the door. Jovita knocked on many, many doors, each time receiving the same response.

I was glad someone was helping us, but inside I was still frantic and anxious. She could not find Mom. Even though she talked to a lot of people, we did not recognize anyone she talked to. None of them were our parents. The more people she asked, the more scared I got. I did not recognize the houses or the streets where Jovita took us. It felt like I was suddenly transported in the middle of a crowd unable to remember how we ever got there.

After walking for some time, my brother, Bobby, started to slow down from fatigue. Jovita finally felt the drag of Bobby's arms, and she knelt down again to look me in the eyes. "Are you sure you live around here, Fernando?" she asked.

I shrugged my shoulders with doubt. "Um…my mom brought us here. I don't know," I said. "Do you think she'll be back soon?"

The nice lady sighed and forced a smile as she squeezed my dusty, tear-stained cheeks together with her soft fingers. "Let's keep looking," she said as she stood and escorted us to the other side of the road.

Several hours later, our search had turned up nothing. No mother and no father in sight. No one she spoke to recognized us, nor did I recognize anyone she asked. We clung to the nice lady like a life raft in a hurricane, for she was the only person who spoke to us or showed any concern at all. As the sun began to set, the situation looked grim, and from the look on her face, it seemed that she was already late for something because of us.

"Come with me," she said with a hint of sadness and impatience in her voice. *The woman wants to help, but she needs to get home to her children, too*, I thought.

I looked at my young, scared brothers and huddled them closer together as Jovita hailed a jeepney (a modified World War II jeep with an extended cab that holds up to ten people) with a yellow and red stripe along its side and the word *Mandaluyong*. Mandaluyong is one of the cities and municipalities that compose Metro Manila in the Philippines.

Jovita said, "Boys, I am sorry. We need someone to help us find your parents, OK?"

I nodded in agreement. I had no choice. We were scared, and I was more scared than my brothers. But I thought Mom would show up again. The ride in the jeepney seemed to go on forever, but new passengers who got into the jeepney and handed coins to pass to the driver for the fare mystified me. Adriano and Bobby were also intrigued by this new scene and all the people who passed us.

Chapter 2

Somewhere Far Away From Home

We finally arrived after what seemed a long ride to find our mother. "Let's go, boys. We are here," Jovita said. I was happy to hear those words. I just knew she knew where my mother was, and I felt reassured that we were going to be reunited with our mom.

"OK, boys, follow me."

I let my brothers out of the jeepney first and followed behind them. We walked into an alley with two brick walls on each side and a narrow path. I did not recognize the road we were walking through and wondered how my mother got this far. We saw kids running around the area; maybe our mother was looking for us here. We approached a chain-link fence. On the right side was a little house with a guard standing inside.

"Hi, can I help you?" the guard asked.

"I need to talk to the head social worker," Jovita replied. "I have children with me who may need her help."

"There, go on, just straight ahead past that flagpole. On your right side is the door."

"Thank you very much, sir," Jovita responded politely.

Of all the memories of my childhood, I remember this moment most clearly. I followed Jovita as she walked toward the flagpole in the center of the circular driveway. In front of us was a building with yellow walls and a large glass door with a sign on top with the single word "Welcome." As my brothers followed behind me, I felt uneasy. I knew I was not in the right place because I saw a group of kids near the building. Jovita opened one side of the glass door and told us to enter.

"What are your names?" the lady behind the desk at the Reception and Study Center asked brusquely, glancing at us.

"Fernando," I said shyly, fighting back tears. I did not know what was going on. "And this is Adriano," I said, motioning to my four-year-old brother who held my left hand, "And this is Bobby," I said, pointing at my two-year-old brother who clung to my right leg. We stood closely together in front of her desk. After Ms. Jovita Mondale explained our situation to the lady in charge, she said goodbye with a smile. I am grateful for what she did for us, taking the time to make sure we were safe.

"How old are you?" the lady asked, filling out paperwork behind the desk.

"Six."

"When is your birthday?"

"Um…I don't know."

"You don't know?" She wrote that down. She asked me where we lived, but of course I did not know that, either. I was frightened. We were in a strange place, and it was getting dark outside. The lady kept asking questions, but I did not know any of the answers. All I could think about was finding my mom. I was far from home and did not even know which direction home was. *How will Mom know where to find me?* I thought.

"Can you help me find my mommy?" I asked innocently.

"We'll try," she replied as she stood up and came out from behind the desk. "For now, you'll have to stay here."

I felt slight relief that someone would help me find my mother, but I did not feel reassured. I was scared of this new place, but at least I knew that someone could help me with my brothers. It was a big facility with lots of kids running around—some older, some younger, and some my age. I stared at them with a mixture of misery and curiosity. We followed the receptionist across the courtyard.

"This is where you are going to sleep for the night." The room resembled a small military barracks with six beds on each side of the walls. There was a room for boys and a separate room for girls.

That night, all three of us cried ourselves to sleep. My brother, Adriano, kept asking me, "Are we going to find Mom tomorrow, Fernando?"

I said, "Sure, we are. Plus, we will have other people helping us tomorrow."

Bobby stumbled out of his bed and leaned over my bed. I put my arms around him and tried not to cry so he would not start crying. Perhaps I tried to replace my mom's arms and to reassure them that he was safe. It was comforting to have him with me and to know that all three of us were together. Still, it was the saddest time of my life and my brothers' lives.

All things seemed uncertain. I had my two brothers with me, and I did not know what to do. I was exhausted from the day's events and fell right to sleep.

According to my adoption records, "On April 15, 1974, Fernando Pineda, Adriano Pineda, Jr., and Bobby Pineda were admitted to the Reception and Study Center for Children, Bago Bantay, Quezon City, Philippines, by Jovita Mondale after having been found in the vicinity of Project 8 where they were abandoned by their natural parents, Adriano Pineda, Sr., and Mrs. Linda Pineda." Years later, when I read this statement from "Fernando's File" that my mom (Rebecca Kuehnel) gave me, I cried like a baby. I did not know where the emotions came from, but I had no control of them. When I read it, I felt like a disposable diaper, discarded when soiled.

The next morning, my brothers and I were awakened by the sounds of squeaking beds and feet slapping the floor. We rubbed our eyes and blinked in confusion before remembering the events of the day before. Our eyes met and our hearts dropped when we noticed that Mama was nowhere in sight.

"Breakfast time!" one of the kids shouted at us as he ran from the room.

Breakfast! I thought. We were starving. We had not eaten lunch or dinner the day before. The thought of food made my stomach grumble. All three of us jumped out of bed, and I raced after the other boys while carrying my little brother, Bobby, so that we would not get lost.

The dining hall was large. Long tables were set up with rows of chairs on either side. We sat on one side, and the girls sat on the other. Adriano and I joined a table of boys and sat down at two empty seats. Somebody walked by and scooped a small portion of cornmeal onto each plate. I reached for this food before one of the boys shot me a warning look. He shook his head vigorously before bowing his head down to his chest.

"Let us pray," called out a voice.

Before we were allowed to touch the breakfast, one of the house parents led the children through a prayer. With my eyes closed and hands clasped in front of me, I silently and fervently wished for my mom to come get us. When it was finally time to eat, all three of us were so ravenous that we ate the meal without really thinking about what it tasted like, and when I was done, I licked the plate. So did Adriano. Then Bobby followed.

After devouring breakfast, we did not really know what to do. We still did not understand where we were or what had happened to us. The other kids had scattered, but I had no idea where they went. Adriano clung to me for guidance.

"Let's go to the front gate," I said to my brother. "Let's see if Mom and Dad came by to get us yet."

When we got to the front gate, a guard stopped us.

"Where are you going, boys? You can't leave the orphanage," the tall man said.

"Did our mama come by?" Adriano asked, squinting to see the guard through the morning sun.

The guard looked down at them. "What's your name?" he asked.

"My name is Fernando, and these are my brothers, Adriano and Bobby."

"No, I don't think your mom stopped by today," the guard answered. "Come and check tomorrow." He looked away.

"My mom will come get us soon," I reassured the guard. "She just got lost yesterday, but once she finds out where we are, she'll come and pick us up."

The guard listened without saying anything. Perhaps he knew something and did not want to disappoint us.

"We'll wait," I said. "Mom and Dad might be here today."

My brothers and I stood on the curb all day, looking anxiously up and down the street. I was certain that my mother would come pick us up that day. I was sure she must have made a mistake and that she had gotten lost the previous day and could not find us. When we got tired of standing, we sat and watched people go by. Some of the kids asked us to play, but I did not want to miss my mom. My two younger brothers wanted to go and play but would not go without me. There was a steady stream of activity in the street; women hurried past with shopping bags, school kids dawdled along in their uniforms, street vendors carried their wares, stray dogs sniffed the gutters, and motorbikes slowly maneuvered through the crowd. A few hours passed, but our parents' faces never appeared.

"I'm bored," Adriano said.

I sighed and reluctantly stood up. "We'll be back tomorrow," I said to the guard. I took Adriano's hand, and we walked back into the courtyard in the middle of the compound, where a small group of kids was playing next to an avocado tree. They stopped playing and watched as we approached.

"Who are you?" asked the oldest boy, who looked about seven or eight years old. He had a shaved head, like all the other boys at this place.

"I'm Fernando, and these are my brothers, Adriano and Bobby. Who are you?"

"I'm Santiago," he said. "Is it your first time here?"

"I'm looking for my mom," I told the kids. "She got lost yesterday when we were out shopping. We couldn't find her."

"I can't find my mom, either," piped up a small girl. "I don't know where she is."

"Me, too," said a little boy who looked Adriano's age. "I'm waiting for my parents to come pick me up."

"Really?" I asked with interest, my eyes wide. "You can't find your parents, either?"

The kids all shook their heads. Some of them looked away sadly and remained quiet. At that moment, it dawned on me that maybe the situation was not quite as serious as I thought, if this place was full of kids looking for their moms and dads, too! Maybe my mom and dad would come by soon to get us. *Maybe it will be OK after all,* I thought, believing this was a place where kids would go if they lost their parents. It was comforting to me that the others kids felt alone, too, and that I was not the only one who cried myself to sleep.

I temporarily forgot about my plight while my brothers and I joined the kids in a game under the tree. But by the time the sun went to sleep and darkness fell, anxiety and loneliness once again crept into my heart.

The next morning, my brothers and I woke up early as the rising sun poured through the dirty windows into the room. I imagined that on this day, my parents would finally come to take us home. In my mind, I pictured my mom running toward me with her arms reaching out to lift me up. Surely she had been frantically searching all over for us. By now, our mom and dad must definitely know where we were…at least that is what I was hoping for.

After wolfing down breakfast, we raced each other to the gate with the same vigor as we did on the first day. Adriano was faster than me and got there first.

"Did our mom stop by yet?" I huffed, trying to catch my breath.

"Not yet. I haven't seen any mom or dad for anyone today," the guard said.

"Oh." My brothers were disappointed.

We sat on the curb again, but this time sitting and waiting was more difficult and boring than the day before. Each passing moment chiseled away my confidence of going home soon. I did not want my brothers to know about the doubts I was feeling. Every time I saw a woman who resembled my mother, who had similar hair or a similar build, my heart started racing as I strained my neck to get a closer look, only to be disappointed when I realized it was not her.

I did not know what to do. I felt so desperate and helpless. Every passing hour on the curb whittled away my hope of seeing my mom and dad.

Days passed in this manner. For several hours a day, I went through the somber motions of our daily ritual: walking to the gate, asking the guard about our parents, then sitting on the curb and staring restlessly up and down the street. I finally allowed my brothers to play with other kids while I waited at the gate. But sometimes Adriano would climb up on brick fence. The fence was more than ten feet tall with broken beer bottles on top designed to keep kids in and strangers out. Adriano took a rock and broke off a section of the glass so that he had a clean spot to sit in. He would sit for hours waiting for our parents. I would walk by to make sure Adriano had not fallen off and then go back to what I was doing. By now, my doubts were getting deeper that my parents would never come, but I did want not to admit it to myself or share that dark feeling with my brothers. I did not want to take away whatever little hope my younger brothers had. Adriano never gave up waiting. I never stopped hoping.

Confused and angry thoughts raged through my head: *Why aren't Mom and Dad showing up? Did we do something wrong? Maybe Mom and Dad don't like me or my brothers anymore.* After spending several futile hours on the curb waiting for my parents, who never appeared, I walked back inside the orphanage with a sense of loss and intense pain that I cannot describe. I hung my head low, kicking up a flurry of dust as my feet shuffled along the ground. At night, when I was sure no one could hear me, I cried silently into my pillow and prayed for Mom and Dad to take us home.

Unable to sleep, my thoughts drifted back to my last hazy memories of life before the orphanage. We had been staying at Aunt Marie's house, which was a nice place with a large orchard full of fruit trees. She let me and my brothers feed the pigs and chickens every day. I loved watching them grunt and squawk as they gobbled up the cabbage and kitchen scraps as soon as we dumped them into their pen. Sometimes this made our bald-headed Grandpa smile as he sat in his wheelchair, quietly watching from the back patio. I thought he was very old, and he never said much, but he seemed nice.

I always thought Aunt Marie was rich because she had a fancy cover that she placed over the fruit on her table to keep the flies away. She even had a refrigerator inside her large, gated house. A brick wall lined the perimeter of her property, with broken glass embedded along the top. "To keep people out," she explained.

My brothers and I stayed at her house for a short time. I could not remember how long exactly, but I remembered that my parents were gone most of the time. My aunt told me that my dad was away, working for the navy.

I tried to remember my parents, but my recollections were fuzzy. I could not see faces. The last thing I remembered was the night my brothers and I were jolted awake by a loud bang. My parents started arguing, and soon they were screaming at each other, saying things I did not understand. I ran into the room as the front door slammed shut again. My dad was outside, storming away from the house. My dad yelled at her to come back, but she did not. Bobby started crying. We all tumbled outside into the dark night. Clouds drifted past a crescent moon; it was extremely dark; only the light from the house lit up the street. It was very late. My dad tried to follow but she kept walking faster and faster. I tried to follow her, but Adriano was holding me crying. It was shocking for me to see my mother disappear into the darkness. I watched her walk away as though burning that moment into my memory. I was sobbing. The street was silent except for my father's shouts and my brothers' cries. I stood outside the front door and watched, wondering what had just happened. It felt like the longest moment of my life, watching my mother disappear into the darkness.

I remembered crying myself to sleep on that dismal night, just as I was doing every night in the orphanage. It did not matter that my home life with my parents was not perfect; I still wanted them back.

My Third Parents

As days turned into months, I no longer spent hours sitting on the curb. My brothers and I still went to the gate every day and glanced out, lingering a few minutes in case we might spot our mom, or even our dad! It had become a habit, one born out of hope and desperation rather than any genuine conviction that something would come out of it. Although neither of us said it out loud, I knew Adriano was struggling with a growing ache that carved a hollow void in his heart. Bobby was in the nursery with the other toddlers. He was too young to be running around with us. He was only two years old, and he needed to be with the toddlers, so Adriano and I were left to watch for our parents. I started to started doubt that my parents wanted us and feared that they did not love me. I felt that they were not looking for us anymore.

With the days dragging on, I began adapting to my new surroundings. In the mornings we attended school at the orphanage and for the rest of the day, we invented games to play with the other kids, climbing trees and shooting marbles. Aside from our daily trip to the gate, our daytime hours were fairly pleasant.

In some ways, the orphanage was not a bad place, especially during the rainy season, because it had food, shelter, beds, and decent showers. Going to school was not so bad, either, because it helped pass the time, and we received a small amount of attention from the teachers. Other than that, we never got much attention from adults. Even though the house parents were nice, there were simply too many kids to look after. The house parents were never able to give the individual attention that many of the children secretly and desperately craved. I know I did.

Although our basic physical needs were met, our emotional needs were utterly unfulfilled. I longed for the comfort and affection of my mom more than anything else in the world. I knew my brothers suffered from the same desperate yearnings—especially Bobby, who had no one to hold him and soothe him when he was crying. Bobby often spent hours lying on the nursery carpet with several other crying babies, but I was rarely allowed in to help him or even give him a hug. It pained me to watch my baby brother from the doorway helplessly, but there was nothing I could do.

The separation from our mother would later tragically affect my brother Bobby. I am reminded of the work of a famous psychologist at University of Wisconsin, Dr. Harry Harlow[1], who was intrigued by love. He found that if he took infant monkeys away from their mothers and instead gave them artificial wire mothers, monkeys that had artificial mothers failed to thrive or even die. However, the young monkeys reared with live mothers and young peers easily learned play and socialize with other monkeys. John Bowly, who studied World War II orphans, has already proved this theory during World War II: infants often died in orphanages, despite adequate nutrition and health. His observation of war orphans proved that without some form of warm, physical contact and comfort, the infants died, despite adequate physical care. But Bobby did not die. In his early twenties, he suffered a schizophrenic breakdown. He had become emotionally and socially secluded from us.

The daylight hours were easier to bear than the long, sleepless nights, which offered no distractions from the terrible mess we were in. I often stared up at the dark ceiling, thinking about my parents. By then, I could barely remember what my home life had been like. I was too young to have many clear memories, so the memories I cherished were often mixed with fantasy and the innocent delusions of a young child's yearning.

I remembered floating on my father's lap in the ocean; the only laughter I remembered with my father was bouncing off the shimmering waves.

"Pretend I am a boat," my dad said. "You are the captain."

"Your boat has a hole—it's sinking!" I screamed with pleasure, pretending to be in agony.

"No, you can't sink me!" my dad said with a chuckle as he tried to push me under.

"Fernando! Adriano! Time for lunch!" my mom called.

---

1 H. F. Harlow, "Development of Affection in Primates, *Roots of Behavior*, E. L. Bliss, ed. (New York: Harper, 1962), 157-66.

I giggled as my dad swiftly twisted around like a fish.

"Hold onto my back," he said. I wrapped my arms around my father's neck as he slowly swam back to shore with me, the sun warming our backs. Mom greeted us as we emerged from the ocean, folding me into a towel like a *lumpia* or egg roll, and holding me briefly before rubbing me dry.

When did this happen? Had I ever really gone to the beach with my parents? I could not be sure. But it was a nice memory and a comforting thought, so I cradled it in my mind like a precious dream and prayed that it would one day become a reality.

"Who wants to be a drummer boy?"

"Ooh, me! Me! Pick me!" we all shouted, thrusting our hands into the air.

It was nearly Christmas. Eight long months had passed since we first walked through the orphanage gates. To me, it felt like an eternity.

To help celebrate Christmas, the house parents organized the children to perform a production of *Little Drummer Boy*. I desperately wanted to be one of the drummer boys, but I was not picked. *Maybe I'm not a good enough actor*, I thought gloomily. I wanted to play the part to feel that I was part of something and everyone would pay attention to me. I felt utterly unwanted. I felt as I felt my parents had rejected me.

I enjoyed the show anyway. Secretly I was wishing I was up there mimicking their regal movements and donning their special costumes. After the performance ended, I waited until everyone left, then I snuck up on stage and pretended to be a drummer boy, waving my arms as if I were beating an invisible drum. "Come they told me, pa rum pum um pum…. I'm a poor boy, too, pa rum pump pum…. I have no gift to bring…." Even though no one was looking, I enjoyed myself on stage because I identified with the drummer boy; really, I was playing for God and my mom. I hoped God would hear me play for him and bring my mom back.

On Christmas Eve, I lay in bed and stared at the Parol, a three-dimensional star made of rice paper and bamboo that the children helped put together and hung on the windows. The fake cheeriness only dejected me further. I did not understand why my brothers and I were at the orphanage. We had parents, after all. *Did my parent's get really lost, or did they leave us on purpose?* I obsessively asked this question in my head. I could not be sure. In a way, it did not matter. If my mom showed up right now, I would hug her and forgive them. I still wanted to be at home with mom and dad more than anything in the world. To be hugged and held, to be loved and looked after—that is all I wished for. That's all we wanted for Christmas. I prayed to God to help me find my mom and cried myself to sleep that night.

Christmas Day came and went, with no sign of Mom and Dad. The sadness that ate away at me every day grew even heavier. We did not receive any presents, but we did not expect any, either. At least I had my brothers. Adriano and Bobby were my only true connection in the world. Bobby was usually in the nursery with other toddlers, but Adriano and I stayed close.

"Dodo?" Adriano whispered. He called me "Dodo" because he could not pronounce Fernando without fumbling it to "Frando" or "Rando." It was a way for him to call me without struggling and being ridiculed by other kids.

"What?"

"When are Mom and Dad coming to get us?"

Night after night, we repeated the same conversation. I did not know what to say anymore. As much as I secretly yearned for my parents, I was now so full of doubt that I could not be sure they would be coming anymore. Yet I always said, "They'll be coming soon. Maybe they'll come tomorrow and take us home." I hated to lie to my little brother, but I did not want Adriano to be sad, so I made up whatever story I could to dry Adriano's tears.

I felt just as sad as Adriano—lost, scared and alone. I put my arm around my brother and hushed him to sleep. We tried not to cry in front of the other kids, so we cried into our pillows. On many nights, I watched my brother's silent sobbing body outlined in the moonlight that shone through the windows while I choked back my own tears.

As we entered the New Year, a dull sense of loss permeated all of my daily experiences, even when we were running around playing kick the can or climbing trees.

The routine was starting to be too much for me. I was barely allowed to see my baby brother, I was sick of going to the gate to wait for my mom, and my heart was weary from listening to Adriano's cries at night. Because Bobby was younger, he looked to me, his big brother, for the love and affection that he wished for from our parents. I tried my best, but I could never be an adequate substitute for the guidance of a real parent. I was a child myself and needed affection, too.

Most of the time, Bobby was with all of the other babies, about a dozen of them. They would be lying on white blankets on the floor or in their cribs, sleeping or staring into space. I could see that the babies were rarely held or given affection, simply because there were too many of them and not enough house parents. I would have happily spent hours holding Bobby and playing with him, but Bobby spent most of his time alone.

On Sundays and Wednesdays, the house parents took us to attend services at a Catholic church. The orphanage's Catholic-based teachings instilled in us both a fear and reverence of God. "Pray and He will answer your calls," the voice called out from the pulpit.

I prayed that God would answer my calls. I prayed before meals and before lying down to bed. When I could not sleep, I prayed even more.

Why wasn't God answering?

One day, Adriano and I were playing marbles in a muddy patch by our cottage. More than a year had passed since we had been dropped off at the orphanage. Time seemed to move slowly for us. The previous year felt like forever, each day without our parents slowly smothering our spirits. We still wore the same clothes we had worn when we were dropped off, so now our T-shirts and shorts were torn and ratty and didn't fit right anymore. Bobby's belly stuck out like a melon, and mine was not much better. We had holes on the heels of our slippers. They were not replaced, so most of the time we walked around barefoot.

While we were playing in the sand one day, a house parent called out to us: "Fernando, Adriano, Bobby! You have a visitor!"

We looked at each other, mouths and eyes open as wide as can be, and leapt to our feet. A visitor? We ran so fast toward the office that Adriano tripped and fell on the path. "Come on!" I shouted excitedly. We reached the office panting.

"Daddy!"

We threw our tiny arms around dad's legs and hips, hugging him. It was as though he had just come home from work. "Dad! Are we going home? Where were you? Are we going with you?" I could hardly believe it. We were going home! It was the happiest moment of our lives.

Dad hugged us back and let out a strained laugh at our questions but never gave us any answers. We were so excited we did not notice. I was in tears. I could not control it. I was smiling and crying at the same time. It was like a day of sunshine with rain. Our joy was overwhelming. My heart burst with elation. I was happy to see my father; my brothers felt that the day had come when our prayers were answered. Many nights we had prayed for this day that every child in the orphanage craved. It was finally our turn to have a visit from our father. We felt proud, like millionaires with the biggest house on the block. The other children envied us. My father played with us with a brand-new plastic GI Joe jeep. This day was better than a second Christmas in the same year! I put my doubt aside and played with my brothers.

My Third Parents

"Have some watermelon," my dad offered, setting Bobby onto the bench next to him. He sliced open a large watermelon he had brought with him, which we quickly devoured. It was delicious. I wanted to finish the watermelon so that we could go home right away.

"When are we going home?" Adriano asked, with watermelon juice dripping down his chin. At first, it shocked me that he would ask, but I was also hoping he would ask that dreadful question. I looked at our father's eyes while he bit into his juicy melon, pretending that he did not hear the question. I waited for his answer patiently.

My father did not answer.

"This is for you, too," he said, pulling out some more toys. Adriano pounced on the plastic GI Joe jeep, pushing it around and around our dad's feet while I jumped up and down, beaming. Some of the kids came over to see what the commotion was about.

"We're going home!" I shouted to the kids as I danced around my dad. "This is my dad; he came to get us!" I was proud to be able to show the other kids that I was not an orphan. I learned later in life that in the Filipino culture, a worse fate than death was not being poor, but being an orphan. It is an indicator of the cohesiveness of your family. Now they could see that we really did have parents and that my father cared about us. He came to pick us up. I thought with confidence. It was such a relief. I felt like God had finally answered my call! I wondered if the other kids watching us were thinking that they, too, would be picked up by their moms and dads.

"Here, I want to give you this," Dad said. He handed us some coins and paper bills from his pocket.

"What is this?" I asked, holding the paper and coins in my palm.

"It is money," my dad said.

"What for?" Adriano asked, peering at the coins. Why would we need money if we were going home?

"You spend it," replied their father. "You need money to buy things."

"Like candy?"

"Yes, like candy. And food, and other things." My father paused. "You need money to get by in the world. I do not have enough money to take care of you boys. That's why they're taking care of you here."

I reflected on this for a moment and then handed the money back to my father. Adriano did the same. I figured that because I did not really know what I could use the money for, and my father said he needed it, he should have the money instead. My dad took the money and put it back in his pocket without saying anything.

"Do you want to see your mom?" he asked.

My eyes lit up. "My mama?" I said in a daze while Adriano shouted "Yes!" and jumped up from the ground. "Where is Mama?"

"We'll have to go into the city. Let me get day passes for you both. Bobby is too young, so he will have to stay here."

Dad went to the office and got day passes so that Adriano and I could leave the orphanage. I felt proud as we walked outside of the orphanage gates, my feet lifting with elation at every step. I was still in tears. My dad had finally come! We were leaving the orphanage forever—maybe we'd never have to go back to that sad, lonely place! On top of it all, I was going to see my mother. It was all too good to be true.

Clinging to my father's hands, the two of us walked deeper into the city, past many buildings. I had never been to this part of the city before. Aside from church, I had not left the orphanage in more than a year. Eventually we walked past all of the tall buildings and arrived at a rickety assemblage of smaller dwellings built with old, unpainted plywood and tin roofs. They were very close together, some right on top of each other. The streets were crowded with people—children playing, women doing laundry, and men smoking cigarettes—as well as stray dogs scurrying around and an odor of burnt fat and oil.

My dad stopped in front of a little house, a shack haphazardly built from old, used plywood. Part of the roof was caving in, and one of the sides was starting to rot.

"Go inside, Fernando," he said. "Your mother is in there."

My Third Parents

My brother stayed with my dad as I stepped in with anticipation and fear, moving from the brightness of the streets to the dark interior of the shack. I blinked to adjust to the darkness. There was very little furniture, and a towel covered a window to keep the light out. I could faintly make out the form of a woman sitting on a chair in the corner. As my eyes adjusted, I recognized the woman—it was Mama.

"Hi, Fernando," she said. "How are you?" She held a tiny baby in her arms. "This is your sister."

I stood where I was feeling uncomfortable. In the house was a man I did not know; he was standing very close to my mother. I was not sure what to make of what I was seeing. I was shocked. I thought of my dad outside the door. It was not what I pictured it to be. I imagined my mother would be happy to see me and that she would be hugging me, but she appeared inconvenienced. I had dreamed of this moment so many times, but it was not turning out like I thought it would. I had no idea what to say or do.

"Hi, Mama," I said finally. I was shocked to learn that I had a sister. *Will Mom want my brothers and me to go stay with her?* I wondered. I was dying to know but could not bring myself to ask. Although I felt happy to see my mom after all this time, the scene in the room confused me. I have often wondered what I saw that day. *What was that scene about? Was that really my sister, and who was that man? Was he her lover? A new husband or a stranger of the night?*

"Are you boys taking care of yourselves?" my mother asked, cutting through my flood of thoughts.

"Yes," I said.

"Come here," she said, beckoning with her hand. I moved closer. She reached out and gave me a hug with her free arm. I hugged her back, clinging to her neck. I did not want to let go, and I started to weep. After a while, she gently pulled away. She handed me ten pesos and patted me on the head.

"Take care of yourself, Fernando," she said. "And take care of your little brothers."

"OK," I said. "I will, Mama."

It was a short visit. There was not much else to say after that. Even though I was dying to know whether my mom would ask me and my brothers to live with her, I was too afraid of what the answer might be to ask. I felt the answer was apparent in that odd scene with a strange man and unknown child in the room.

I joined my dad and my brother back on the busy street. My dad didn't want to have my brothers see my mom. I wasn't sure why. May be he didn't want my brothers to remember her so they won't have to yearn for her. I had all kinds of questions, but the look on my dad's face told me not to ask anything about my mother. I reached for my father's hand and decided to keep quiet about what I had seen in the house. I am not sure why my father took me there to see my mother. Was it to persuade her to come home with us? Did he think maybe seeing me might change my mom's mind about being with that strange man? I asked myself these questions later, but as an eight-year-old boy, I did not say anything. I wanted to protect my father's feelings.

"Are we going home with you today?" I asked Dad as we continued walking.

"I'm working to get some money," he said. "When I have enough money, I can take you out of the orphanage."

"Yay!" We were satisfied with this news. We bounced down the street with our dad. Even though we were heading back to the orphanage, we were so happy that our father had come to see us that we were walking on clouds the whole way back. We had high hopes that he would take us home that day.

When we reached the orphanage, we were once again led through the gates. This time we felt OK because our dad was there, and we knew where we were going. Adriano ran back to his toy Jeep and began to play with it again. My dad knelt in front of me. He had a serious look on his face that told me something bad was about to happen.

"Fernando," he said solemnly, "I want you to promise me something. Will you help me take care of your brothers while I am away? "

"OK, Daddy," I said. I felt proud that my dad was giving me this responsibility, which I had been doing already. Yet part of me worried it did not make sense. There was something odd about the tone of his voice. "I will be back for you guys very soon. I promise," he said with a smile. All of a sudden, that mysterious, odd feeling went away. I was happy that he gave me the responsibility to care for my precious brothers, and I wanted to make him proud.

I remained hopeful. "You come back soon to pick us up, OK, Daddy?" I screamed to my father.

"OK," my father said. "I have to go now."

"Do you have to?"

"Don't worry. I'll be back soon," he reassured me.

"You promise?" I added.

"Yes, I promise." My dad uttered that last word slowly.

The three of us reluctantly walked back to the gate to say goodbye. We did not want him to go. After final hugs, we stood and watched our father's back as he walked away until he got swallowed up by the crowd and disappeared. He turned around once to look back at us and waved. We wept with the same overwhelming feeling of sadness that we had felt when he first arrived at the orphanage.

The next day, Adriano and I went straight to the guard after breakfast and asked, "Did you see our dad? Our dad came to see us."

"Yeah, that's good," the guard said. "Did you have fun yesterday?"

"Yes!" I said. "So you just keep on looking for my dad, because he said he will come back for us."

"Yes, I'm glad he will be coming back." The guard said this with no change in his tone of voice. He did not seem confident about saying it. But I was certain that my dad would be coming back because he said he would. He promised.

Every morning from then on, I went to the gate, and Adriano climbed on the top of the brick on the same spot with renewed hope that our dad would show up to take us home. After a few minutes of looking up and down the street, I went back to play with the other kids. Toward the end of each day, I went to the gate again to ask the guard if dad had come by. The guard always answered, "No, not today."

Walking away, I said to myself, "I know he will come for us one of these days. He said he would come and take all three of us home."

We were happy for a while after our dad's, glowing with the thought that he would come back to get us. Our happiness lasted about a month before it faded, along with the distant memory of that special day with our father.

After a year, my dad still had not returned. The toy jeep he had brought us was now gone, broken from use by other kids. I still ventured toward the gate, but not every day anymore and never twice a day. I would walk over and stand a few yards from the gate area, glancing at the street from a distance, unwilling to get my hopes up by advancing farther.

Josefina J. Fernando, a social worker from the orphanage, went to our grandfather's house, but no one answered the door. She was not sure if it was empty or if the relative choose to ignore her, knowing that she was looking for our parents. When a personal search failed, registered letters were sent to the last known addresses of my mother and father. The social services received no response. Our photos were printed in the newspaper, to see if anyone would claim us like lost luggage. According to my adoption records, not a single phone call was received and nobody stepped forward. The printed notes in my file read "On June 13, 1976, after exhaustive efforts to find the boys' natural parents, but proved futile, the '*patria potestas*' of their natural parents were terminated by the government." My brothers and I were officially alone, unwanted, kicked-out, and officially the property of the government of the Philippines. We were legally and officially declared abandoned and neglected.

My Third Parents

I was filled with terror.

"Do we have to go?" I asked.

"Yes, you have no choice."

Bobby shrieked and grabbed my arm. I was dizzy from fear.

"But why do we have to go? We didn't do anything wrong!"

"You are too old. RSCC is for young kids, and Nayon ng Kabataan is for older kids," the house parent explained. "You can't stay here anymore," she said, turning away. "We are taking you to Nayon Ng Kabataan in five days."

My heart dropped as I blinked back tears and shivered with fear. The words of the house parent were like a death sentence. The reputation of Nayon ng Kabataan was well known among the orphans as a hostile place filled with big, mean kids and nasty, uncaring house parents. Some kids said we would be better off in the streets than in Nayon.

As soon as the house parent left, several kids rushed over and taunted us: "Ooh, you are going to Nayon ng Kabataan!! You will get beaten up, and the other kids will take away your food! The house parents are mean. They will whip you and hurt you…and the food is awful!"

I was nearly ten years old. For the next five days, I was jittery with anxiety and dread at the thought of going to Nayon. I wished and prayed that my father would come pick us up right now, before they moved us to the other orphanage. All I could think about every day and every night was all the awful things the kids would do to us, and I doubted I could protect my brothers. Every morning for the next five days, I went to the gate, feverishly looking for my dad. "Please, please come right now and pick us up," I prayed as I looked up and down the street.

This is all my fault, I thought, closing my eyes as I leaned against the fence surrounding the orphanage. *But I didn't do anything wrong. I'm not a criminal! So why are they punishing me and my brothers like this?*

Most of all, I feared for my brothers. I was the oldest; Adriano was seven, and Bobby was only five. The kids at Nayon would be much older and bigger. I would have to defend my brothers and watch out for them. I had promised my dad. *I'm not a criminal*, I thought again and again. Every time I saw the house parent, I asked over and over why we had to go and whether we could stay at RSCC instead, but the answer was always firm.

Every orphan who did not get picked by his or her parents was labeled as "abandoned." So that's what we were—abandoned.

Prayer has been my savior and shield from the sanity and cruelty of my childhood life. One of the most helpful miracles in my life was how praying helped me cope, even though I thought my prayers were never answered.

I prayed for a miracle. I could not sleep; I was too scared. I cried and prayed for my mom to come and pick us up. I prayed that somehow she would find out that her sons were moving to a very mean, nasty place where they could get hurt. Maybe if I prayed hard enough, she would show up the next day and rescue us. Surely she wouldn't want me and my little brothers to get beaten or go hungry, would she? After endless hours of silent weeping and pleading to God for help, I fell asleep just minutes before the house parent came to wake us up.

The sky was still dark when the house parent said, "Fernando, Adriano, Bobby—time to get up," tapping us on the legs. "Take your things. We're going to Nayon ng Kabataan today."

I had prayed that the night would never end, but it did. I reluctantly climbed out of bed, hoping that the sun would not rise at all that day. Maybe it would stay dark forever, and we would not have to go.

"Fernando, pack your things, and then help your brothers pack," the voice called from down the hall.

I moved extra slowly, shuffling my feet as if they were made of lead. I helped my brothers, but they didn't have much to pack—just a couple sets of shirts, a few pairs of shorts, and their sandals. I finished packing and paused, closing my eyes one last time for a silent prayer. Adriano walked up to me and whispered, "I am sorry. It is my fault. They are sending us to Nayon because I stole the gerber. I was hungry." I was shocked that he was blaming himself for something that had happened months ago.

"Adriano, it's not your fault. It's mine," I said softly, grabbing my brother by his shoulder.

"Fernando, time to go!"

I opened my eyes and sighed. It was time to leave, and our mom and dad had not come to rescue us. I had no choice. Shuffling my feet, I walked out of the cottage with the thought that my life was about to change again.

Dread filled every bone in my body.

This is a photo of Adriano, me, and Bobby in 1978, a year after arriving in the second orphanage, Nayon.

Chapter 3

Nayon Ng Kabataan

I walked out the front gate of RSCC feeling like a prisoner heading toward his execution. My footsteps sounded heavy on the sidewalk, and I struggled not to cry.

Don't panic, it will be OK, I kept telling myself, although I did not believe it.

Adriano, Bobby, and I followed the house parents through the streets, walking away from our second home in four years. I felt like I had years earlier, walking to house after house looking for my mother, stunned at being abandoned. I was leaving my house mothers, friends, familiar faces, the routine that we had grown to expect. I wondered if I would ever see those children again, and I feared the children I was about to meet. Most of all, I was scared for my younger brother, Bobby.

The streets were noisy and loaded with motorcycles and jeepneys painted with pictures of the Virgin Mary and Jesus in flamboyant colors. We boarded a jeepney. Normally we would have been laughing with excitement to do something novel like ride in a jeepney, but not on that day. We climbed onto the long seats in the back and squished together for the long ride to Kabataan. The jeepney could fit twelve in the back, but the adults had to slouch or else they would hit their heads on the roof. It was cramped, and every time we hit a pothole, we bounced from our seats. The journey seemed endless, and I had time to consider every possible new misery awaiting us. Bobby sat next to me clutching my hand, and I worried about how I could defend my little brothers from mean kids. The bright designs on the jeepney glimmered in stark contrast to the dark clouds looming overhead; looking at them only made me feel gloomier.

The jeepney made many stops throughout the city; people climbed off while others piled on. I wished we would ride the jeepney forever and never have to get off, but this hope was quickly shattered when the house parent abruptly rose from her seat and ushered the three of us out the back of the vehicle.

As my feet touched the ground and I looked around, I felt almost dizzy; I was so disoriented by the new location. We had arrived in an unfamiliar side of town, and from there we had to walk the rest of the way to Kabataan. We three boys followed closely behind the house parent as she maneuvered down a busy road lined with traffic. Along the way, I stole glances at my surroundings. This was certainly not the prettiest or cleanest side of town. The trash-strewn street was lined with dilapidated store fronts. Hordes of people hurried past in both directions. Plastic bags and torn newspapers tumbled along the road, thrown into the air from cars zipping past. The noise of the traffic was unnerving. Nevertheless, my thoughts fled ahead to the fate that was awaiting us.

We had nothing to hold onto for safety as we stepped through this unfamiliar world. Inside I was screaming *Help me!* and sobbing, but no one heard me, not even God. No sound escaped my lips as tears rolled down my cheeks. I felt overwhelmed by fear. My brothers and I had only each other and the light sacks that carried our few belongings. We had nothing to give us comfort or reassurance, not even the house parent who we obediently followed. We rounded a corner and came to a large, fenced-in area—the orphanage. We entered through the big, double, chain-link gate at the front. The house parent spoke a few words to the guards and then motioned to us. Taking a deep breath, we stepped inside the compound.

I held Bobby's hand as Adriano walked on his other side. Silently, we took in our surroundings as we followed the house parent to the reception area. The place was huge and filled with kids running around. Some of them stopped to size up the newcomers. I eyed the other kids and feared for my younger brothers, worrying that some of these older kids would beat them up once they got the chance. I thought about what dad had said, "Butch (Fernando), you have to take care of your brothers because you are the oldest." Would I be able to protect them?

Looking at the other kids, I noticed the face of a large teenager slouching against a tree. He had a long, jagged scar on his cheek, and as we walked past, he smirked at us. I quickly averted my eyes and looked straight ahead, fighting back tears. I knew that crying would be fatal. I did not want to show weakness or fear to the other kids, so I wore the most stoic expression I could muster. Adriano also stood firm, pretending he was not scared. He was bigger than me at that point and seemed to welcome battle. I was not as concerned about Adriano because he knew how to fight. But Bobby was young, small, and did not know any better, so he cried openly, freely divulging the terror that we, his older brothers, also felt inside. I held him close.

Inside the reception building, the house parent from RSCC gave the receptionist our files and exchanged a few words with her before unceremoniously departing. Our last connection to our previous orphanage was gone; we were now on our own to fend for ourselves in this new orphanage.

The receptionist introduced herself as Ms. Santacruz. When she opened her mouth, the words shot out like fireworks.

"Hello, boys. What are your names?"

I thought that information would be in the files she had briskly whipped open, but I answered anyway.

"OK, boys," she said. "We have rules here, and you have to follow the rules or you will pay the consequences. To start with, you cannot leave the orphanage. Is that clear?"

Before we had a chance to nod, she continued. "Your house parents are in charge. Follow the house parents' rules and you should not have any problems. We will put you to work—you will earn your keep. No objections and no exceptions. We do punish insolence, laziness, and bad behavior, so make sure you do as you're told."

We stared at her wide-eyed and silent as she rattled off a seemingly endless list of rules. A cold shock of fear ran down my spine as we listened to her high-pitched, authoritative voice. *Maybe those kids were right about what they told us*, I thought. She eyed us over the top of her glasses.

"We offer several different programs. There's stuff you can do here. You can learn music, go to school, attend half a day of school. You will have things to do, so you do not need to leave the orphanage, and if you do, you will be punished. Do you understand?"

We nodded. She ushered us out of the reception area and walked us to a cottage.

"You boys will be sleeping in the same cottage. We're keeping you three together."

I felt a slight rush of relief at the news, but it was not enough to alleviate the tightness in my chest.

"Here you are, in Cottage 3. Fernando, you will have to take care of your brothers here."

Her words echoed the last words I remembered hearing from my father those distant years ago.

"These are your beds," she said, pointing to three empty beds made of gray metal with a two-inch spring attached to it. A flat sheet of metal had been laid across the springs, and a thin mat rested on top of that. There were two rooms in the cottage: one smaller room containing three bunk beds and another room with eight bunk beds, all lined up like a military formation.

"You have closet space over here," she continued crisply, opening a closet door. The closet was already filled with the other kids' things, so Ms. Santacruz shut the door and said, "There's not enough closet space to go around, so you'll have to share or keep your stuff under your bed. Understand?"

We nodded.

"As I said, stay out of trouble and obey your house parents, and you will be fine," she said. She marched from the room, leaving us alone with the handful of boys who had stood in the room silently watching the newcomers.

I looked around the room. The other boys were snickering at Bobby's sniffles.

"Let's go explore the orphanage," I said to my brothers. I was uncomfortable in that room with those boys and could not wait to get out of there. I wanted to get a grip on these new surroundings. I plopped our sacks on our beds, uncertain whether any of it would even still be there when we got back, and then took my brothers' hands and left the cottage. The three of us were glad to get away from those kids. We had not even met them yet, but they did not seem very welcoming.

Together we walked around the orphanage compound and tried to get situated. There were eight cottages: two for girls and six for boys. In addition to the reception building, there was a mess hall for eating, a central auditorium that appeared to be used for church services, and a platform that looked like it could be used for performances and cultural dances. There was also an infirmary and some buildings that housed classrooms.

This orphanage was much larger than the previous orphanage, with about 250 children from ages seven to twenty-one—except for Bobby; he was only five. My brothers and I kept our distance from the older, bigger kids as we surveyed our new surroundings. Most of the kids were bigger than us. I was small for my age, but Adriano was bigger than me and also bigger than a lot of the other kids. Bobby was so young and small that he would be an easy target for bullies. How would I manage to protect my younger brother? At least Adriano was big enough to defend himself.

All in all, we had been taken care of fairly well in the previous orphanage, where the kids were all younger and the facilities were nicer. Judging from the looks of things, Nayon ng Kabataan would be a lot rougher than the RSCC, where we first learned what it meant to be orphans. I was about to realize that the bad things we had heard about Kabataan were all too true.

When we returned to the cottage, the boys who had been there earlier were gone. There was just one boy in the room now, flopped on a bed. He sat up as soon as we came in.

"Are you new?" he asked.

"Yeah," I said defensively, bracing myself.

"I'm Sonny," the boy said. "What's your name?"

"I'm Fernando, and these are my brothers, Adriano and Bobby."

"Do you have any candy?"

We each said no. *Why does he ask?* I wondered. *Does he want to bully it off of us if we do have any?*

"Well, if you have any candy, don't show anybody."

We did not ask why.

"If you have candy, eat it now or hide it; otherwise, you'll never see it again." Sonny flopped back on the bed and then asked us some more questions. The way Sonny spoke, I could tell that he had been in orphanages for a long time and had a lot of experience in places like Kabataan, even though he was only two years older than me. He brimmed with confidence and did not seem the slightest bit scared of anything. He spoke in a matter-of-fact way that reassured me.

Sonny seemed nice. The more we chatted, the more I felt like I may even be able to trust Sonny. I was relieved to have met someone at the orphanage who was not threatening and did not want to take advantage of us. Maybe Sonny and I could even be friends.

I was settling down to sleep on our first night at the new orphanage, trying to find a comfortable position on the hard metal bed, when Bobby appeared and crawled into bed with me. He was crying. "When is Mommy coming to pick us up?" he whispered.

"Soon," I lied, putting my arm around my younger brother. "She'll be here soon. Just go to sleep now." Bobby wrapped his arm around me, and I hugged him tight to me. There was a comfort and safety in our embrace. It was sort of a substitute for a mother's affection.

I felt sorry for my five-year-old brother. I knew that Bobby could barely even remember Mom and Dad. He never got to experience much affection or the soothing sensation of a gentle, parental touch because he was alone most of the time at the first orphanage with all the other babies. When Bobby got too old to stay in the nursery at RSCC, he stayed with me, and I was given the task of taking care of him. Even though I was just four years older than him, I was the closest thing to a parent that Bobby ever had.

As I lay in bed holding my crying brother, the reality started to sink in that our dad was not coming back—but I refused to stop hoping. Our dad had come to visit us in the other orphanage, after all. Maybe he was just trying to save enough money to take us home, like he said the last time we saw him. I wondered if our mom would be the one to come get us. I wondered if our parents knew that we had moved to a new orphanage. I said several fervent prayers then quietly cried myself to sleep.

At 7:30 the next morning, the bell rang for breakfast, jolting us awake. It was so loud that Bobby fell out of bed. Luckily we were on bottom bunks.

A few boys laughed and sneered as Bobby picked himself up off the floor. I glared at them.

In the dining hall, the chaos and chatter died down as another bell rang and all of the children knelt down at once in a line facing the Virgin Mary picture on the wall, then prayed before breakfast. The smell of frying cornmeal wafted from the gas stove outside the cottages. After quick prayers, we all sat down and wolfed down the food in seconds flat as soon as it appeared on our plates. I was still hungry, but there was not enough for second helpings. Bobby was slower in eating, and some of the kids snuck up and snatched some of his cornmeal.

"Get away, you assholes!" I hissed, swatting at a boy whose hand appeared out of nowhere to swipe Bobby's cornmeal.

"Fuck off," the boy said, slapping me on the head before returning to his seat. He returned to a table of laughing boys, licking the few bits of stolen cornmeal from his fingers. I wanted to cry but could not risk it. I knew that if I showed weakness, I would be targeted. I was a sensitive boy. I had to learn to hide these feelings.

"Don't touch my brothers" Adriano said as he stood up menacingly from his chair, but the other kids just laughed at him.

I put my arm around Bobby and guarded his plate. "Hurry up, Bobby," I said. "Eat quickly from now on so that those scumbags don't get any more of your food."

Bobby looked at me gratefully. His wide eyes welled with tears as he finished his food. The kids had stolen at least half of Bobby's cornmeal, but since there wasn't enough left over for seconds, he would just have to get by until lunchtime.

After breakfast, we attended a half day of school, but it was hard to concentrate. There were so many students that the teacher was not able to give each one individual attention, so he was not able to find out at what level of schooling we three newcomers were. We were each completely lost in our lessons, and as a result, we were bored and easily distracted. I was interested in learning but could not keep up, so I spent most of the time secretly examining the other kids in the room and silently praying for one of the house parents to rush into the classroom with the news that our parents were there to pick us up.

Lunch was a bland, meager affair that left my stomach still grumbling. It was often soup with Chinese cabbage and rice. Fish and meat were rare treats. There wasn't enough food to go around, so I just silently clenched my stomach and tried to think of other things, such as going home. Food was so scarce that kids often stood by the fence and waited for the other children outside the orphanage to tease them. The outside children with parents would taunt the orphan children: "Losers... nobody wants you, loser!" Then they would throw loaves of bread and tamarind candies over the fence to watch everyone dive over the food, kicking and pushing each other to get a piece of the prize. The outsiders would laugh watching the orphans fight for the meager food. Then they would tease us more: "Losers...your whore mother is never coming back."

In the afternoon, we were put to work. Toward the back of the compound was a garden, which was one of the food sources for the orphanage, even though the harvest was obviously meager. The boys were made to till the hard, dry soil with a hoe and pick in an effort to ready the impenetrable black earth for planting. I did not understand how anything could possibly grow there.

By dinnertime, I could barely walk, and I was covered in dirt streaked with sweat. My brothers and I stumbled into the mess hall, eager for food.

"Is this all?" Adriano said, looking forlornly at the tiny chicken leg and small array of vegetables on his plate. It was down his throat within seconds.

Dinner was nothing special, and it was nowhere near enough to fulfill our hunger pangs, but at least it included that one small piece of chicken. I held Bobby's piece of chicken tightly while he ate his vegetables to make sure none of the other kids stole any more off of his plate. Then I devoured my chicken in a few bites, cleaning off all remnants of meat from the bone. I was still hungry, so I fiddled with the leftover chicken bone in my hand. I noticed other kids cracking their chicken bones and sucking out the marrow. I tried it, too. I cracked the chicken bone, sucked out the marrow, and chewed the cartilage. It was quite tasty, but I was still hungry.

I was sweaty and filthy after a long day at school followed by working in the garden in the Philippine heat.

"Where are the showers?" I asked Sonny after dinner.

"Showers?" Sonny laughed. "Come with me."

Sonny led me and my brothers around to the side of the cottage and pointed up at the rain gutters. "See that?" he said. "When it rains, that's where you will shower."

I stared at him, dumbfounded. "You don't have real showers here?"

Sonny shook his head.

"Well, what do you do during the dry season?"

Sonny shrugged. "There's a sewer in the back of this place."

"A sewer?" I shuddered. I was hot, dirty, and sticky from the day's sweat, but I sure did not want to bathe in a filthy sewer. I thought back to the group showers at the RSCC and realized how luxurious that place was in comparison to Kabataan.

The next day, I had no choice. After I worked in the garden again that afternoon, the house parent complained that I was dirty, and the other kids teased me about smelling bad. I prayed for rain to fill the rain gutters so that I could shower using water that fell from the sky, but the clouds failed to come. Reluctantly, I went over to the sewer at the back of the orphanage, stripped off my clothes, and washed in the foul-smelling water. It was more like a rinse, though, because I did not have any soap, but at least my skin was no longer black from the dirt.

Life at Kabataan was tough. Everything we had feared was now a reality: the violence, the lack of food, and the cruel house parents. Just getting through each day was a struggle.

We were constantly hungry, our stomachs still rumbling after every meal. After a while, our stomachs learned not to rumble, but nothing eased the constant ache. The meals usually involved rice and some kind of soup, such as Chinese cabbage soup, but it was always pretty bland. Breakfast was always cornmeal and sometimes a banana. We ate everything we were given, from bones to banana peels, because we were still hungry. Even if food dropped on the ground, we ate it. On the lucky days when we got a piece of fish for dinner, we ate the eyes of the fish, sucked out the brain, ate the tail, and licked our plates. We ate everything that could possibly qualify as food, leaving nothing at all for the insects to eat.

The garden that we toiled in every day was nowhere near big enough to feed the entire orphanage. If it would have been fertile enough to grow more food, I would have volunteered to work day and night tending that garden so that I'd have enough food to fill my stomach, but it just wasn't possible to grow anything substantial in that tough ground.

After my afternoon shift digging the soil, my feet were black with dirt. Our shoes had worn out, so we were barefoot most of the time. The orphanage did not have the means to buy the kids new shoes or even to give us used, donated shoes. Because we had nothing to protect our feet, we had to run from the paved road to the grass to prevent our feet from burning on the blazing asphalt. The hot ground caused our feet to crack. Over time, our feet got so hardened that we would not even realize when we had stepped on a sharp rock unless we saw blood dripping on the floor.

I was grateful that Kabataan at least had toilets. There was never any toilet paper, though. We had to use water from the toilet to clean our butts. Only sometimes was there soap around for us to use afterward. I relished rainy days because it meant I could have a shower under the rain gutter. Fresh, clean water was a luxury because it was so rare.

The sewer in the back of the orphanage often overflowed and turned into a little lake with schools of tiny fish. We orphans were so hungry that we tried to catch the tiny fish, desperately fashioning makeshift fishing poles out of sticks or trying to scoop them up in our tattered shirts. Everyone had scabies, but we did not realize that we got it because the water was mixed with the flooded sewer system. Sores appeared all over our bodies, infecting our genitals and armpits the worst. Every day, the kids picked at our sores and peeled the scabs, shooing away flies until we got so tired of it that we just let the flies land on our open lesions. One day, Adriano came down with a fever after swimming in the dirty water, and he just curled up on his bed all day. Once a month, we all lined up to have our heads shaved; otherwise, we would be full of head lice.

Besides the lack of sanitation and other basic necessities, every day at Kabataan was a fight for survival. Violence and bullying were common. My brothers and I never bullied anyone, nor did we join the groups of kids that would gang up on other kids. It just was not part of our nature. Instead, we spent most of our time defending ourselves and trying not to get beaten up, which was both tiring and demoralizing.

I received my share of bullying at Kabataan, but it was my younger brother, Bobby, who bore the brunt of the other kids' violent, sadistic tendencies. More times than I could bear to count, I watched helplessly as older kids physically abused him. I never stood by idly when I saw this going on—I did all I could to stand up to those nasty kids. I shouted, I hit them, I flung myself on their backs, all to no avail. Nearly everyone in the orphanage was bigger than I was, and I was also outnumbered. Any time I stood up to the bullies, there was always someone to push me back.

One day, I heard a commotion inside the cottage, followed by Bobby's desperate shouts for help. I raced inside and saw two kids swinging Bobby by his hands and feet. With brutal gleams in their eyes, they swayed him back and forth like a toy while the other boys in the room laughed viciously.

"Put my brother down!" I screamed as I threw myself at the bullies. When the boys released Bobby, his body was tossed against a metal bed frame, and he was knocked unconscious. Two other kids pounced on me immediately. One kid punched me in the jaw, pushing me to the ground and knocking one of my right upper teeth out. The other boy kicked me in the stomach and called me names as I gasped for air.

When Bobby regained consciousness, the boys who had been swinging him laughed harder and tossed him into the air like a ball. Bobby's head smacked against the corner of a bed with a sickening thud. He passed out again.

Adriano rushed into the room and swung his arms at the bullies. He was a big kid, so a couple of the boys backed down, except for one defiant kid named Jake, who lived in the cottage next door. Jake picked up a 4 ft. by 4 ft. plank of wood that had a bent nail sticking dangerously out of one end. He smacked Adriano on the head and fled from the room. Blood spewed from the wound, but Adriano steadied himself and ran after Jake. When he caught him, he beat the shit out of him as a circle of kids gathered to watch.

I cradled my brother, Bobby, yelling over and over for help from the house parents, but no one came. Bobby's head was bleeding all over my hands. I did not notice it at the time, but I was also bleeding from my mouth. My missing permanent tooth would be a lifelong reminder of that day. The room was empty. I held my brother and called his name, begging him to open his eyes.

Finally, a house parent angrily pushed through the crowd of kids watching the fight.

"What's going on here?!" she demanded. "You!" she said, pointing at Adriano, "Get yourself to the clinic—now."

"But you gotta check on my brothers!" he yelled. "They're in the cottage."

Adriano ran back inside the cottage, the house parent close behind. Bobby groaned and opened his eyes, which immediately filled with tears from the throbbing pain in his head. The house parent carried Bobby to the infirmary as Adriano and I followed closely behind.

Bobby was bleeding from the back of his head. His hair was bloody, and blood was dripping to the ground. We followed the blood trail to the infirmary in tears. Our spilled blood and tears mixed on the ground, and I felt an indescribable emotion of fear, guilt, and anger. Adriano followed, cursing angrily. Bobby carried this scar on the back of his head for the rest of his life. The nurse said he probably had a mild concussion. Adriano's cut was bandaged, and he, too, earned a permanent scar from the day's altercation.

After the nurse treated our wounds, the house parents grilled us for information about what happened. They wanted to know who started it, who was involved, and how it unfolded. As I retold my version of events, I melted into tears when I got to the part about Bobby being tossed into the air. The house parent grimaced.

"All right," she said. "You three can go. You're in the clear."

Later that day, the house parents found Jake. He had been hiding in the back of the cabin to avoid punishment. It was pointless hiding because there was nowhere to go, and he knew he would be punished. He came out when the bell rang for dinner. His left eye was black, and his lower lip was cut and swollen from the fight. Instead of letting him eat, the house parents ordered him to take off his clothes. He refused. A male house parent stepped forward and slapped him, then yanked off his T-shirt. Jake grumbled and pulled away, quickly taking off his shorts and underwear.

"Pick up this chair!" the male house parent barked.

With his head bowed low, Jake picked up the chair and held it in front of him.

"Higher—hold it higher!"

Jake lifted the chair awkwardly until the house parent pulled it straight up above his head.

"There. You keep that chair over your head, and you march in a circle around the orphanage. Do not stop marching. You need to think long and hard about what you did and why you're not getting any dinner tonight!"

After dinner, Jake was still marching naked as ordered, holding the chair over his head. The other kids piled out of the dining room and watched, laughing and taunting him, knowing that they were safe with the house parents there. My brothers and I watched silently from afar and then retreated to a quiet circle of trees in the far part of the complex, where we could temporarily escape from the madness of the orphanage.

"I hate this place," Bobby said, sniffling.

"I know," I said. I put my arm around him. "I do, too."

"When is Mommy coming to get us?"

"I don't know. I think she'll be coming soon," I lied and squeezed him harder.

I was exhausted. How many more days like this could I handle? Kabataan was sapping my energy, draining me emotionally and physically. Try as I might, I could not always help my brothers. With 250 kids in the orphanage, we were not monitored well, and a high level of violence was unfortunately a regular occurrence.

Every night, Bobby climbed into my bed for comfort and security. We could barely fit on it together, but we cuddled anyway because Bobby was so scared. He cried every night for our parents, even though he could barely remember them. Perhaps some instinct told him that there was more to life than what he had experienced so far—that there was kindness in the world somewhere, even if it was always just out of reach. The only real kindness that Bobby ever knew came from me and Adriano. His attachment to us grew stronger with each passing day and each new ordeal.

I loved my brothers deeply, especially because my father's last words to me burned in my mind: "Take care of your younger brothers because you are the oldest." Although the image of my dad's face faded with time, his parting words remained etched in my psyche forever.

I felt depressed, empty, and lonely as I watched my little brother trace circles in the sand. I could not protect innocent little Bobby. Adriano was living in isolation with other bigger kids in Cottage 6. It troubled me to see Adriano being called stupid and ugly by the other kids, including the girls. However, I could not do anything about it. I was helpless. Yet it was my responsibility to protect my brother from all kind of harm. I could not cope with such a huge responsibility. It was too much for a ten-year-old. I would often confide in Sonny, but he could tell if I was feeling down.

"Hey, Fernando," he said one day, walking up to me.

"Hey," I said, barely looking up.

"Can you get me an empty soup can?"

"What for?" I asked.

"Never mind, just get it. Trust me, you will see. And bring me your old slippers."

"The ones with holes?"

"Yes."

"OK...." I searched the back of the kitchen and dug an empty soup can out of the garbage. I took it over to Sonny, along with my old slippers from RSCC, which were now falling apart.

"The can is still dirty inside. Clean it out, and I'll go get a piece of barbed wire and some other stuff."

I returned with a clean can and watched with wonder as Sonny rubbed the bottom of the can against the ground. The friction wore out the seal on the bottom of the can, so now he had a sturdy, hollow tube. Using a scavenged nail and a rock, he made holes in the can, through which he strung a piece of wire. He fashioned wheels from my old slipper and attached them with a string. I watched in awe as Sonny deftly assembled the materials. When he was done, he handed me the string.

"Pull it!" he said.

"What is it?" I asked.

"Pull it!" Sonny repeated, grinning.

So I pulled the string and watched in wonder as the little tin can rolled along on a set of makeshift wheels.

"Hey, it's like a car!" I shouted.

"That's right!" Sonny said. He laughed and ran along beside me.

There were no toys at Kabataan. When the kids wanted to play, we used our imaginations to create our own toys and games. Through a bit of resourcefulness, trash became treasures and provided hours of entertainment.

Bobby watched and cheered as I raced around, pulling the toy car behind me. Sonny smiled.

"Here, this is for you," Sonny said to Bobby, handing him a crushed bottle cap. Bobby's eyes widened as he stared at his treasure. He looked up at Sonny, grinning.

Bottle caps were a hot commodity in Kabataan because we did not get cola very often—only when friends or family came to visit, which was rare.

Bottle caps became the currency of the orphanage. The kids flattened the bottle caps and traded them for marbles and other found objects.

Bottle caps also had other uses. They could be fashioned into cutting tools by rubbing both sides on the pavement to sharpen the edges. This meant that bottle caps could also be dangerous weapons; some kids walked around with sharpened bottle caps in their pockets. Kids like Sonny also knew how to fashion the bottle caps into yo-yos by poking holes in them and stringing a length of thread through them. I wished I could make a yo-yo for Bobby, but I did not have a second bottle cap.

Bobby did not mind. He turned the bottle cap over and over in his small hand, happy to have something he could call his own for a short while, until a bigger kid eventually bullied it from him.

The orphans at Kabataan were fiercely competitive, always trying to outdo or outtough one another. Because we never received any positive reinforcement from adults, we all suffered from low self-esteem. We felt worthless, so we had to prove to one another that we *were* worth something. For that reason, the teasing and taunting often escalated to dangerous levels.

One day, I desperately tried to reach the branch of the mango tree that hung over the edge of the outdoor auditorium stage. "You can't do it! You're too small!" the kids shouted. The crowd of kids roared with laughter while the older kids sneered at me.

"Yes, I can! I can reach!" I shouted with determination.

I ran and jumped, stretching out my arms as far as they would go. All of the other kids were doing it; they could jump off the ledge and swing on the branch like monkeys and then fall effortlessly to the ground. It looked really cool. I was small for my age, so I was not able to reach that elusive branch, no matter how hard I tried. Regardless of how high I jumped, my fingertips only lightly brushed the branch every time. Of course this provided the kids with endless entertainment and amusement. They derived a wicked pleasure from taunting me about it.

My Third Parents

"Shorty!"

"Shrimp!"

"Look, he's so short that he can't reach the branch!"

I fumed at the kids' words and felt my face go red with anger and humiliation. They were no better than me. Anything they could do, I could do, too, and I was determined to prove it.

After a while, the kids grew bored and left. I found myself all alone on the auditorium stage. Fueled by rage and driven by defiance, I decided to race from one end of the platform toward the overhanging tree limb. I walked toward the end of the stage to get a running start, giving me fifty feet of runway. Then, I ran as fast as I could and leaped into the air. I felt the branch in my hands and even wrapped my fingers around the branch! I held on to the branch for a few split seconds of sweet victory, but the momentum of my leap propelled my legs so high I was almost parallel to the stage. My hands were not big enough to grip the branch firmly enough, so I flew through the air, landing on my left arm and hitting my head on the concrete.

No one knows how long I lay there unconscious on the hard cement. No one came by to check on me. It might have been hours before I finally opened my eyes, blinked groggily, and looked around. As I picked myself up, I saw my arm. White bone jutted out through the skin at a 90-degree angle, making a U shape. I panicked at the sight. I screamed as loud as I could while running to the infirmary. I kept screaming for help until one of the house parents came running to see what was wrong.

The house parent took me to the clinic, where the nurse put a large gauge on the top of the gapping hole where my blood was pouring out like a rusted leakey pipe. It was not the pain that made me scream. It was horrifying shape of my arm which was no longer straight and limpy like a broke branch handing in the wind. She said it was, simple break, but it wasn't. It was broken and nothing simple about it. She said, "You'll be OK. Let me get a bandage and get you to the hospital." The clinic nurse quickly wrapped my arm with gauze to stop the bleeding. I was moaning in agony with pain, but I felt less scared once the deformity was covered with gauze.

The guard called a taxi. There were no ambulances or private cars. It felt like forever until the car finally arrived. I stared out the window, wondering what would happen to me next at the hospital.

I was excited to get a cast. I thought it was cool because it was a symbol of my victory. I did it—*I got the branch!* In addition, best of all, I had proof: my arm was in two pieces. I was proud. Now those kids could not taunt me anymore because I had evidence that I could swing from that branch.

I got to stay in the clinic for a week while my armed healed, which was another unexpected treat. I felt pampered because I did not have to work the garden or go to school. I got to sleep all day, my food was delivered to me in bed, and the nurse took care of me. I felt like a king. For that wonderful week, I slept well, and the kind nurse treated me better than the house parents ever did. I was tempted to try to break my bones more often.

That week gave me a nice vacation away from the other kids. Adriano, Bobby, and Sonny came by each day to talk to me. They were in awe of my story about swinging from the branch. Reaching that branch was a major win for me—the kids never teased me about it again. The victory cost me, though; I could not move my left arm for a while, and I will carry the scar from that fall for the rest of my life. But it was worth it.

Even the major victory of my broken arm was short-lived. After a week, I returned to my normal life at the orphanage. I felt as if I had been thrown back into a den of hungry lions.

The kids at Kabataan were not just competitive or antagonistic; they could also be sadistic. The really mean ones formed gangs, and some of the weaker ones latched on to the gangs just because they did not want to get picked on.

The gangs were always coming up with clever ways to bully and abuse the other kids. Not long after I broke my arm, I walked into the cottage to find Sonny convulsing on his bed while the other kids roared with laughter.

I ran over to Sonny's bed and saw that the kids had wrapped a wire around the metal bed frame and then stuck it into the socket. Sonny was being electrocuted. I could not even touch him without getting electrocuted myself. With my heart pounding, I grabbed a pillow and used it to push Sonny out of the bed. Sonny was on the top bunk, and it was a long fall to the floor. The kids laughed even harder.

The next morning, I woke up with burning eyes and stinging lips. I screamed—I thought my face was on fire! The pain was agonizing. Someone splashed water on my face, and after a few minutes I was just barely able to open my eyes enough to see. My lips were raw and throbbing, and my eyes were swollen and aching. I could hear laughter and rude remarks directed at me, but I was in too much pain to care. Adriano brought another cup of water to help wash my face.

"What happened?" I asked my brother.

"Those kids rubbed hot pepper on your lips and eyes," Adriano said, putting his arm around me. "They held me down so I couldn't stop them. Thankfully, Bobby was out playing, so they only got to you." He led me from the room, shooting dangerous glances at the bullies, but unable to retaliate.

It was useless to try to tell the house parents what was going on because if anyone told on a gang member, the gang members would get their revenge later. The pranks they pulled were dangerous and violent, and they did not need to be instigated any more than they already were.

If there was one redeeming thing about Kabataan, it was Sonny. We were developing a solid friendship. The ability to trust someone was a ray of sunshine in my otherwise squalid life. In Sonny, I saw my own reflection to a degree; here was another kid about my age who had been stuck in orphanages from a young age, a kid who was decent and moral, a kid who was just trying to survive in a hostile world, a kid who managed to survive years of indescribable hardships and challenges without succumbing to negativity or lashing out against others. The only difference was that Sonny had more street smarts, perhaps because he simply had more experience living the hard life.

Sonny and I were moping around one day after lunch, trying hard to ignore our growling stomachs, but we could not.

"Let's go to the garden," Sonny suggested, "and see what we can dig up!"

"I don't know," I said. "Isn't that stealing?"

"Nah, it's all right," said Sonny. "We work here, after all. We have a right to those vegetables…right?"

"Um, maybe."

After making sure no one was looking, we snuck into the garden and ran over to the nearest plot to stick our fingers into the ground, pulling up a tiny carrot that had not yet matured.

"That's tiny!"

"I don't care, I'll eat it!"

Suddenly we were yanked to our feet by one of the male house parents.

"What do you think you're doing?!" he roared.

"Um, we're just hungry!" whimpered Sonny.

"Yeah, we're really sorry, we just wanted something to eat," I said.

"You know you are not allowed to dig up food from the garden," the house parent reprimanded us sternly. "Can you imagine if all of you did that? There would be nothing left in the ground!"

"We're sorry, we're really sorry." We stared at the ground, trying to act as sheepish as possible.

"Pull down your shorts, both of you!" the house parent ordered.

"But—"

"Do as I say!!" he barked.

Slowly Sonny and I lowered our pants.

"Now lie flat on the ground," the house parent said. We obeyed.

With my face pressed into the dirt, I let out a yelp as the house parent whacked me across my bare butt with a long, flat stick. Thwack! Thwack! Sonny started screaming, too. Thwack! Thwack!

This went on for some time. We were so used to being whipped by the house parents that it did not really hurt anymore, but we all pretended to cry just so that the house parent would stop.

"Please," Sonny wept. "We're sorry, we're sorry!"

"We won't do it again!" I wailed.

"Get up," ordered the house parent. "Pull up your shorts."

I stood and gingerly pulled my pants over my sore, stinging bottom.

"We're not done yet," said the house parent. Sonny and I eyed each other behind his back. Sonny rolled his eyes.

The house parent led us to the back of the kitchen, where he ducked inside and grabbed a bag of salt and spread it on a small but concentrated spot behind the kitchen. Hundreds of thousands of grains of salt lay scattered across the ground.

"Kneel in the salt," the guard said.

"What?" asked Sonny?

"Do as you're told!"

I slowly lowered myself to the ground and gingerly knelt on the salt. Sonny did the same. The house parent ordered us to stretch out our hands, palms up. He placed a brick in each one of our hands and made us kneel there, in the salt, with bricks on our hands for hours. After a while, the salt rubbed into our knees, causing agonizing pain. My hands and arms throbbed with the weight of the bricks. While we groaned with misery, the house parent sat casually in a chair and whittled on a stick. Sometimes he left for a few minutes, and we would rest our hands. As soon as the guard returned, we quickly picked up the bricks again.

It was a horrible punishment for the crime of trying to feed our constantly empty stomachs, but we were used to it. Every time the guard left, we rolled our eyes at each other and shook our heads. We knew that there was no way out of this punishment; we just had to bear it.

It was effective, though—we never stole food from the orphanage garden again.

I was eleven, and I had been at Kabataan for more than a year. One day, Sonny and I lay on our beds, trying to cool off from the stifling summer heat. A few of the older bullies were lingering in the room, talking in low voices in the corner. I was certain that they were up to no good. I apprehensively kept one eye on them, in case they tried anything, so I was completely surprised when they suddenly stood up straight, dropped their mean expressions, and adopted shy smiles, staring at the door with wide, innocent eyes.

As the door opened, the strangest people I had ever seen walked into the room. They were tall and fat, with light-colored hair and white skin. Some had blue eyes, and some had green eyes. There were four of them: two men and two women. They looked around the room and smiled kindly at the boys. The house parent followed them in.

"Boys, these are visitors from the United States," she said. "They have come to view the orphanage and say hello to you all."

"Hello!" said the tallest, fattest one. He beamed at the boys. "Nice to meet you!" he said to no one in particular.

The normally fierce bullies mumbled "Hello" in soft voices and batted their eyes at the white women.

"Would you like some candy?" one of the ladies asked the bullies. The normally savage boys nodded placidly as the white lady stepped forward, placing a sugary sweet into each of their palms. She turned around and gave a piece of candy to Sonny, who was also acting as cute as possible, before offering one to me with a kind smile. I just stared with my mouth hanging open, still unnerved by these white people. I had heard of white people, so I knew they existed, but this was my first time actually seeing them! It was like they came from another world, especially with their clean clothes, fat bodies, and the freshly washed scent of soap that entered the room with them. One lady wore a straw hat. Her face, which I guessed was normally white, was covered in red splotches, and she furiously waved a fan in front of her perspiring face. She gave me a strained smile.

"Now, let me show you the girls' cottages," the house parent said, escorting the white people from the room. The bullies immediately followed at a respectable distance.

"Who were they?" I whispered to Sonny in awe.

Sonny laughed. "They're Americans. They come to the orphanage sometimes to look around. It's good when they come because they give us candy and quarters and stuff like that, and the house parents don't beat us for a while."

"Wow," I said, chewing on my candy. I made sure to eat mine right away so that no one else would get it. Sonny expertly hid his piece of candy in a hole in his mattress.

"Come on," he said, getting up. "We can keep an eye on the white people and try to run into them later."

The white people did not come that often, but when they did, I made sure to act as cute as possible.

One evening, I was wandering around the orphanage with Sonny and my brothers when we heard a strange sound. We went over to investigate.

"What is it?" Bobby asked.

"Shhhh!" Sonny said, stopping in his tracks. The others bumped right into him. "Look!"

He pointed at a thin cat that was walking on top of the brick fence between their cottage and the neighboring cottage. It was the first and only time we ever saw an animal at the orphanage. Most animals seemed to have a sixth sense that the kids were desperately hungry, so they stayed away. Maybe this cat was too stupid to realize that. It was a scrawny and scruffy creature, with its ribs visible through its matted fur, but we did not care. It was food!

As silently and stealthily as we could, we picked up rocks from the ground.

"On the count of three," whispered Sonny. "One, two…three!"

A barrage of rocks hurled through the air. The cat did not notice until it was too late. With a terrible shriek, it fell to the ground, unconscious. We leapt on it and beat the cat to death without any hesitation or hint of sentimentality. We carried their prize to the back corner where no one else would see us and started a small fire. My brothers and I kept watch while Sonny prepared the cat, then slowly twisted its broken body over the small flame. When it was well roasted, we quickly tore it apart and gobbled it down.

"That was so good," I said, licking my lips.

"I wish there was more," Bobby said.

"We're gonna starve to death in this place," Adriano said.

"We don't have to," Sonny said.

Everyone looked at him.

"What do you mean?" I asked.

"Well, we could sneak outside and find food," Sonny said matter-of-factly.

"Huh? How?" Bobby asked.

"Yeah, how would we get out?" Adriano asked.

"There are ways," Sonny said mysteriously.

"We'd get caught and whipped," I said nervously, although I secretly relished the idea.

As hungry as I was, at that point I would rather cook and eat a stray cat than sneak outside the orphanage to find some food. The outside world was tempting, but I was afraid to leave the orphanage because, as violent and horrible as it was, it was our safety zone. I did not know what lay outside the orphanage grounds, but it would not be long before I found out.

At night, I never stopped praying for my parents through my silent tears, hoping they would come to get us so that we could be a family again. By this time, I had forgotten what it was actually like to be with them—whether it was as wonderful as I imagined or not. But my fantasies were all I had to comfort myself, so I clung to them.

Every day, my brothers and I stood by the gate, as we had at the RSCC, and hoped to see the figure of our mom or dad appearing down the street, coming to get us. Sometimes I thought maybe my aunt would show up. But our parents never came to Nayon ng Kabataan. Neither did our aunt. I began to think we would be living there permanently, but I never got used to it.

The everyday violence and abuse at Kabataan wore the orphaned kids down. Some of the kids became hardened, and most of us lived in constant fear. Although the conditions were terrible, it was all most of us had ever known, so in some ways we did not actually realize how bad it was. I always dreamed of something better, but I did not know how to get it. One thing was obvious: I would never find happiness, let alone the path to a better future, by staying at Kabataan.

The perimeter of Kabataan was lined with a brick wall with barbed wire and broken glass on top. I was not sure if that was to keep outsiders from coming in (not that anyone would want to), but I definitely knew that it was to prevent us from getting out.

As time dragged on, I began to wonder more and more about life beyond the orphanage. The confines of the orphanage wall were starting to suffocate me and stifle ads I hoped for a better life. I grew curious about what opportunities might be out there.

I realized that if I really wanted to, I could escape. A few weeks earlier, Sonny had shown me a small hole in the fence in a far corner of the orphanage compound. But what would I do on the outside?

The house parents who ran the orphanage did not want the children to escape and always threatened us with harsh punishment if we did, but they never actively prevented the kids from leaving. In fact, the front gates were always open. Yet no one ever ran out the front gate because we all knew we would end up starving to death on the streets. As bad as Kabataan was, at least it promised some form of shelter, a meager amount of food each day, and some form of identity and sense of community, no matter how dysfunctional and abusive it might be. Life in Kabataan was better than being an anonymous street urchin…at least it had been for a while.

It was not long before curiosity got the best of us. At Sonny's coaxing, he and I snuck out of the orphanage together a few times through the hole in the fence. We walked around for about half an hour at a time, keeping our secret trips short so that the house parents would not notice. Sometimes we would get lucky and find five pesos lying on the street, so we'd pick it up and buy some candy, then sneak back into the orphanage through the secret hole.

"Wouldn't it be nice if we never had to go back to Kabataan?" Sonny wondered out loud, chewing on half a piece of candy. He had given the other half to me.

"Yeah," I mused. "But how would we survive? Where would we sleep? How would we get food?"

"Yeah, that's the problem…." Sonny's voice trailed off.

I relished these short trips into the real world. These brief bursts of freedom were the only thing I really looked forward to anymore. One day Sonny and I slipped through the hole in the fence after we had received a peso each from some Americans who had come to visit the orphanage. We raced to the store a couple of blocks away and bought a few pieces of candy, which we devoured on the way home. Complacently, we wiggled back through the hole in the fence and came face to face with the cold stare of a house parent.

"You know you're not supposed to leave the orphanage!" she yelled.

We looked at the ground, pretending to be ashamed. We had been caught; there was no way we could lie our way out of this one. We knew what was coming.

She marched us over to a table inside one of the empty classrooms and made us lie down on the hard table top. With a long stick, she whacked our bare butts until they were red. Then she forced us to kneel on salt for an hour with our hands outstretched in front of us.

I was sick of these beatings. I'd had enough of the meager food and was tired of all the constant violence and bullying at the orphanage. I did not want to rot in the orphanage forever—I wanted to *be* somebody.

Lying in bed that night, I debated leaving Kabataan forever. I was torn. The possibility was tempting, but how could I survive out there? I knew I was just a kid. I knew that I would have no shelter and no source of food, so I felt I had no choice but to stay in Kabataan, even if the house staff members were really mean and the other kids picked on me.

Plus, I could not leave my brothers. I cared about them more than anything in the world. I would not be able to help them if I ran away. For a long time, I felt I had no choice but to stay there and deal with it, despite the difficult conditions. But after more than a year at Kabataan, a life on the streets actually started to seem more appealing.

The next day, Sonny was gone. His bed was empty that morning, and he did not show up for breakfast. He wasn't in class, and he didn't appear for work. I went to sleep that night hoping that Sonny would pop up the next morning, but he did not. His bed remained empty. I looked in the closet. Sonny's few possessions were gone. I asked some of the other kids, but no one knew where Sonny had gone. He had simply vanished.

Eventually a new kid was assigned to Sonny's bed. He was not as nice as Sonny, and it was not long before the new kid joined the gang of bullies, to my despair.

Sonny's absence made the days at the orphanage even less bearable. I wandered the perimeter of the orphanage more and more often, eyeing the hole that we had crawled through so many times. I wondered what kind of fate might await me beyond the fence. A few months rolled by, each one more depressing and difficult than the last.

One day while I was getting a cart in Pasay City, I was greeted with a huge surprise—I saw Sonny! He was at the Recyclable Center office. He raced up to me and pulled me aside.

"Guess what?" Sonny said, bustling with excitement. "Guess where I've been?"

"What? Where?" I demanded. I was shocked and overjoyed—Sonny had been gone for months.

"Out there…." Sonny nodded toward the hole in the fence. "Working!! You should come with me!" He lowered his voice to a whisper. "I know a great place where we can make money!"

I stared at him in disbelief. "How?" I whispered back.

Sonny glanced around to make sure no one was looking and pulled me closer toward him.

"I know someone who can help you. You can get a job where I work, collecting things and selling them. It's fun! You can make enough money to eat and get candy. You don't have to be stuck here anymore!" Sonny's eyes were bright with enthusiasm. "Fernando, you can survive out there!"

"For real?" I said. Sonny's excitement was infectious, and I could not help grinning back at him.

"Yes, for real," Sonny said. "Where do you think I've been this whole time? Let's go right now!"

Right now! My mind reeled with the sudden news. This was a lot to take in. Leaving the orphanage? Surviving on our own on the outside? Could it be possible? I was not sure, but I trusted Sonny. I had fantasized about escaping from Kabataan for so long. This was the perfect chance. But what about my two younger brothers?

"Wait here," I said to Sonny. "I need to tell my brothers I'm going."

Sonny grinned. "Hurry. I'll wait for you here."

I dashed off to find my brothers. I was torn because I felt so responsible for them. On the other hand, I needed to live my own life. I could not watch out for them forever. The responsibility was too big. The allure of adventure was too tempting, and Kabataan was too awful. As tough as it was to leave Adriano and Bobby, I needed something new. I needed to put myself first for once.

"Adriano," I said, pulling my brother away from a group of kids. "I'm leaving."

"What?" Adriano said, looking alarmed.

I swallowed and quickly continued. "I'm going to go outside and see if I can find Mom and Dad. I'll bring them back here to get you and Bobby."

"How are you gonna get out?"

"There's a hole in the fence behind Cottage Six," I explained. "Kids go in and out all the time."

"What?" Adriano's eyes widened. "Don't leave, Fernando!"

"It's OK," I said. I looked away. "I'll be back. I'm gonna go see Mom and Dad and tell them where we are."

"Well, at least take me with you. I wanna come!"

"No, you gotta stay here and watch over Bobby," I said firmly. "We can't leave him alone here. He needs you."

Adriano looked worried.

"I gotta go." I wanted to get this goodbye over with as quickly as possible before I changed my mind. The longer I talked to my brother, the more my resolve crumbled. I had to leave now or else I never would. "When you see Bobby, tell him I'll be back soon with Mom and Dad, and then we'll all go home."

I hugged my brother quickly and then raced off before Adriano had a chance to respond.

"Let's go!" I said to Sonny.

We crawled through the hole in the fence as the sun started to set. I was glad to have my friend back. As we walked away from the orphanage, my feet felt lighter and lighter with every step. The sense of adventure was exhilarating; the sweet taste of freedom was intoxicating. The unknown future seemed to hold such promise. *I had no idea what I was heading into.*

Chapter 4

The Streets

Along the way, Sonny explained how we would make money. "At night we'll collect bottles, copper, stuff like that. Then we'll sell it and make money!"

That sounded interesting and easy enough. Finally I felt like I was about to *do* something. I was taking my fate into my own hands. I was only eleven years old, but I did not have to depend on anybody! It was exciting, and I momentarily forgot that I had brothers. I could make it for myself. I felt happy; it was a feeling I had almost forgotten.

Sonny and I walked farther into Manila, much farther than we had usually ventured during our short escapes from Kabataan. I barely noticed the hot asphalt burning into the bottom of my hard, cracked, bare feet. As we walked, a rare yet familiar aroma nearly knocked me off my feet. The strong smell of chicken legs, barbeque pork, fried squidballs, and other culinary delights wafted seductively from the stands of curbside food vendors, hanging in the air like a succulent cloud of temptation, drawing me away from my intended path. I could feel my mouth watering as I gazed longingly at the tubs full of salty deep-fried peanuts, buckets of pig intestines, and stacks of fried chicken on sticks. It was more food than I had seen in the past five years. I would have been happy to stand there all day just inhaling that wonderful aroma, but Sonny yanked my arm. He, too, was hungry, but neither of us had any money, so we just kept walking.

We walked and walked all day, Sonny leading the way. I followed apprehensively, unsure of where Sonny was taking me. We walked so far away from the orphanage that I worried I would have no way of getting back if

I changed my mind. Trailing after my friend, I stared at everything, overwhelmed by the people and places I had never seen before. *So this is life outside the orphanage*, I thought. It was a whole new world—completely different from sitting around looking at the cottages and the house parents at Kabataan all day. This world was full of possibilities, not to mention food, but what dangers did it hold? Would we be bullied and beaten by these new faces we passed? Who would we sell things to? Would other kids try to steal what we found like the children in the orphanage stealing any bit of food they could?

Finally, we reached a very small house with a lot of cardboard, metal, and covered boxes piled and strewn around the front.

"This is it!" Sonny said. He walked in confidently and said hello to the people who were sitting inside, then turned around and introduced me.

"This is my friend—his nickname is Butch," Sonny said. "He's gonna be working here with us."

Sonny and some of the other kids had called me Butch in the orphanage, and perhaps it was just as well not to give these people my real name.

He turned to me and said, "This is our headquarters. These people own the junk shop next door." I looked around the house, which took only a few seconds because it was just one room, no more than 10 ft. by 11 ft., with the cooking area and living quarters all in the same room.

"This is the family we'll rent the cart from. That's Susan." Sonny nodded toward a middle-aged woman who was preoccupied with a small child. "And that's Jack," he said, pointing to a tall, skinny man who was seated on a tattered chair. "He's the one who will weigh your cart every night and pay you. And these are some of the guys we will be working with," he said, turning toward three teenagers who were lounging in the room.

"Hey, Butch," said the oldest one, who looked to be about fourteen. "I'm Joseph. You can call me Joe. Has Sonny told you the basics of what you will be doing?"

I nodded.

"Good. I've worked here for three years, so tonight I will show you the route you'll be taking."

That evening, as the sun went down, the shops began to close, and the streetlights turned on, Sonny and I followed Joseph around the city.

"First, you'll rent a cart like this from Jack," Joe explained to me while pushing a long, wooden cart. The cart was about as long as I was tall, and it was empty. "Jack runs this recycling business. Your job is to push this cart around the city and sort through garbage to find stuff that is usable or recyclable. You will pick up stuff like cans, copper, plastic, aluminum, metal, and wire."

"What happens to the stuff I collect?" I interrupted. "Why would anyone want that stuff? It is just garbage."

"No, it's not," Joe said. "It can be reused. We have to create our own resources, so we reuse everything we can. Everything is worth something, even if it just looks like garbage."

I let that sink in. Joe continued.

"Sometimes you will work in a team, and sometimes you will be alone. You have to start late at night, because that's when people throw out their trash. Then at the end of the night, you take the cart back and sell the load that you collected to Jack, the guy you just met who runs the junk shop. You will get paid according to the weight of what you have collected." Joe pushed the cart as he spoke. I trailed close behind him, hanging on to his instructions.

As we walked, Joe explained that people dumped their garbage right onto the street, which garbage collectors shoveled into a truck the next morning. The trick was to get to the garbage pile before the truck got there and before the other street kids had a chance to pick through it. The garbage was collected twice a week, so on the nights before each garbage collection, we would have the best chance of finding usable stuff.

Joe wheeled the cart straight to a large mound of garbage. The stench was overwhelming, but Joe and Sonny seemed not to notice as they dove right in, tossing aside handfuls of putrid vegetable peelings and other rotting waste and emerging with a few gems, such as a solid copper pipe; coils of aluminum, which have greater value and weight than pieces; and half-eaten fruit, which had greater immediate value to us because it fed our hunger for the evening. I watched them for a moment before following their lead. I gingerly reached my hands into the garbage pile, half afraid of what I'd have to touch, and pulled out pieces of trash that were dirty, torn, stained, soaked, and rancid. I did not find that much useful stuff, but Sonny and Joe seemed to have sharper radars because they kept pulling out all kinds of recyclables and tossing them into the cart.

"Don't worry, you'll get better at it," Sonny said, digging out a piece of wire. I leapt back in disgust after a container of used cooking oil spilled all over my feet.

"Look for shiny stuff," Joe advised, pulling a half-eaten apple out of the smelly pile. He inspected the apple, wiped it on his dirty shirt, and ate the remaining half. I shuddered.

I learned a lot that night. Joe had been doing this job for many years. He knew exactly where to find the best piles of garbage in the city that we could pick through. Even though the job was stinky and disgusting, I was glad to be doing something as the moon rose higher over the city—something other than lying in my metal bed at Kabataan and crying myself to sleep.

Several hours later, I pushed our cart up to the junk shop, exhausted after my first full night of picking through garbage.

After weighing the load on my cart, Jack reached into his pocket. "OK, that's thirty-five pesos' worth of stuff. Minus twenty pesos for cart rental. That's five pesos for each of you three boys." He handed a few coins to us.

It was the first money I had ever earned by working, but I was too exhausted to feel excited about it. I was not used to staying up until 4:00 a.m.

"Where do we sleep?" I asked Sonny and Joe after we had been paid.

"Anywhere you can," Joe replied. "Here, there, anywhere. Just try to stay out of people's way."

At that moment it dawned on me that I would not have any proper shelter. We really were on our own.

I watched Sonny scavenge a piece of somewhat clean cardboard and lay it flat on the ground by the side of the road. Sonny lay down on top of it and fell right asleep. I gazed down the street, which was littered with garbage and the sleeping bodies of street kids just like me. Some slept in their push carts, while others slept under small makeshift huts with plastic tarp roofs. Most kids slept on the ground like Sonny. With a sigh, I ran off to find my own cardboard and made my bed right next to my friend.

As I lay down to sleep, I said a fervent prayer, begging God to protect my brothers in my absence. I prayed that I would find our mom and dad soon. When I told Adriano that I was going to find our parents, I meant it. Even though our parents had abandoned us five years earlier, I never truly believed that they purposely left us. I still believed that it was all a big mistake and that we were lost. Somehow, living on the streets would bring me one step closer to finding them. Before falling asleep, I prayed that I would run into my mom and dad after I woke up.

I awoke a couple of hours later with the sound of traffic and the movement of footsteps near my head. It was morning; the rest of the world was waking up. A massive garbage truck rumbled slowly down the street as the garbage men swept the trash into the back of the truck. I looked over at Sonny, who was fast asleep on his cardboard "mattress." I tried to curl up and sleep, but it was not comfortable. The ground was too hard. There was too much noise. I was self-conscious about all the people, especially kids in their crisp white school uniforms, rushing past me. What would they think of me? I tried not to care. *Will I see my mom out here?* The thought kept me awake until the blinding light of the hot afternoon sun burned into my eyes. When I closed my eyes, I could see nothing but red. I eventually succumbed to exhaustion and fell asleep listening to the noise of the street.

Hours later, I woke up to quiet. The noise on the street had died. The sun was setting, and the vendors were packing up. Sonny was gone. I was alone.

I slowly sat up and lifted myself up from the concrete. My back was stiff, and my head was sore from sleeping on the hard ground. I was groggy and disoriented because my body had not yet adjusted to its new schedule. As my stomach rumbled, I suddenly remembered the five pesos I had earned the night before. I pulled the money out of my pocket and looked at it.

I did not know how I felt as I held the coins in my hands. I was happy to have some money—five pesos was more than I'd ever had in my hands at one time. On the other hand, I had worked hard all night. Five pesos was not going to go far. It would be enough for one meal, at least.

Remembering the streets lined with food vendors we had passed the day before, I dashed off to see how much a piece of barbequed chicken would cost. I had enough for a leg of chicken, which I devoured in seconds. It was delicious. I licked my fingers and sucked the marrow out of the bone, just as I had done at the orphanage.

It was late evening; there were still several hours to kill before starting work. I wandered by the junk shop, but Sonny and Joe were not there. I did not know where they were. Loneliness crept into my heart. I had not really talked to anyone all day, other than the chicken vendor, but that did not count. As I meandered aimlessly through the unfamiliar streets, I suddenly missed my brothers with a terrible intensity. How they were doing? Were they OK? Were they thinking about me? I prayed that no one was beating them up and that they had enough to eat.

When I showed up for work that night at 10:00, Sonny and Joe were still not around, so I took the cart on my own. I had memorized the route Joe had taught me, but I was not having much luck finding stuff on my own. Most of the large piles of trash were gone, replaced with new, smaller piles. As I looked forlornly at a measly pile of trash where there had been a huge mound the previous day, I remembered hearing the garbage truck that morning. I would just have to try harder if I wanted to make enough money that night to pay for the cart rental and have enough left over to buy food.

After checking the spots from the previous night, I wandered the streets looking for other piles of garbage. Whenever I spotted a pile of garbage, I dug right through to the bottom. Most of what I found in the garbage piles was indeed garbage, but occasionally I found some things I considered treasures. After picking through a pile of greasy food wrappers and crumpled napkins, I uncovered a pineapple. My spirits lifted. I was famished; it had been hours since I had eaten that single chicken leg. The pineapple was brown and felt mushy in my hands. I turned the pineapple over and noticed white fuzz growing near the bottom. I did not have a knife with me or else I would have cut it open then and there, so I carefully rested the precious pineapple in the wooden cart and continued on my way.

As the night wore on, I did not have much luck finding recyclables, but at least I was managing to find a bit of food to eat. I had been disgusted the previous night when I saw Joe devouring a half-rotten, half-eaten apple that came from the bottom of a trash pile, but now I was doing the same thing without giving it a second thought. At that point, I truly understood that when people are hungry and have no other means of survival, they do whatever they have to do to stay alive. Eating garbage was what I had to do.

Most of the time, though, the trash was just trash. At one point, I came across a neatly folded paper bag that had no visible tears or stains. I thought I had really found a prize—only to be met with the sickening stench of rotting shit. I was disgusted but amused, and I laughed. If there had been anything in my stomach, I might have vomited. Because it wasn't garbage night, and perhaps because I was still new at this, I did not manage to collect a lot of recyclables that night. Still, I made four pesos, which would be enough for me to eat the following day.

As I was leaving the junk shop, I ran into Sonny.

"Hey! Where have you been?" I asked, grateful to see my friend.

"Oh, around," Sonny answered vaguely. "I had some stuff to do. You looked through the trash tonight?"

"Yeah, I made four pesos."

"Not bad for being new at it. Keep it up; you'll learn how to find the good stuff."

"Yeah, I guess so," I paused. "Hey, where do you go to get cleaned up? And where do you go to take a shit?"

"I'll show you," Sonny said. "Follow me."

As I followed Sonny through the streets, I kept one eye out for anything valuable on the ground while the other kept close watch on where we were going. I was glad to see Sonny again, even though he'd only been gone for less than twenty-four hours. I was worried that Sonny would disappear for months again and I'd be all alone on the streets. I was beginning to realize that although Sonny was my friend, he often did things on his own. Sure, we were good buddies, but I knew I would never be as close to Sonny as I was to my brothers. We each had our own problems to worry about.

"Here we are!" Sonny announced as they approached a bridge. Instead of walking over it, Sonny led me underneath the bridge, where I discovered a whole new side to living on the streets.

Under the bridge, dozens of kids were sprawled along the concrete lining the riverbank. Some of them were sleeping on cardboard or newspapers. A couple of teenagers were openly masturbating, oblivious to everyone else. A cluster of kids took turns sniffing a bottle of glue, while another raucous group drank from slim, dark bottles.

On either side of the bridge, large drainage pipes emptied into the river. A young boy about my age stood underneath the pipe stark naked, washing himself in the pouring water. Nearby, another boy squatted at the edge of the concrete, with his bare bottom hanging over the river as he added to the waste-infested water.

The stench of the dirty river, mixed with old human and animal feces and stale urine, stung my nostrils. As my eyes swept to the left, I was curious to see two young boys swimming in the river. On second glance, I could see that they were not really swimming—they were treading water as they sifted through the thick, floating mass of debris that surrounded them. They, too, were looking for recyclables.

I watched it all silently and shuddered. This was my new life, like it or not.

I quickly fell into a routine, picking through garbage all night until 4:00 a.m. and always finishing before dawn. After work, as the sun rose on the horizon and the city stirred, I took a shower to wash off the grime and stench of the night's work; the only problem was, the water actually stank as much as the garbage I picked through. The first time I stood under the flow of water pouring out of the city water supply that ran under the bridge, it was a refreshing, free shower. I wondered if the leaks where the water escaped the pipe were made by other homeless children. I learned to ignore the other kids under the bridge, the ones who were sniffing glue or masturbating. The glue sniffers often motioned for me to join them, but I always pretended not to notice. After rinsing myself in the dirty water, I found a spot in the street to spread my sheet of ratty cardboard. The hard ground was uncomfortable, but I always fell asleep within minutes, completely drained from the night's work. When I woke up in the evening, I was always covered with flies because of all the dirt that clung to my body.

As I lay in the road, kids passed by me, and people went about their daily business, stepping right over me as the ants and flies crawled and buzzed over my sleeping body. They did not even look at me; it was like I was a stray dog or cat in the street. I felt that they simply looked *through* me, as if I were a crumpled piece of paper being blown about by the wind.

In the late afternoon or evening, I woke up and brushed away the flies and ants, then checked my pocket for the few pesos I had earned the night before. Those few pesos paid for my breakfast, which was really more like dinner because I ate it in the evening. All of the money I made from my hard work the previous night was spent on that one meal, which was never enough to get me through the day. To survive, I had to rely on the half-eaten, half-rotten food that people threw away.

Whenever I found something halfway edible in the trash, it was like stumbling upon a treat. I'd carefully sniff the discarded fruit, peel off the dirty half, and then eat the other half. I learned to rely on this free source of food. I could not afford to be picky; my life literally depended on it. Mold, dirt, and chew marks were no deterrents. I ate anything that was still edible.

My Third Parents

After a long night of work, I usually made only about five pesos, and that was considered a *good* night's work. There were times when I'd excitedly haul back a cart full of stuff, struggling under the weight of big chunks of metal that made the cart heavy, and I'd get all excited. But even then I was never able to earn an income that could do more than just feed me for a day or, at most, for a few days.

When I was not working, I wandered the streets, mostly alone. I had nowhere to go and no real way to pass the time other than to roam around while doing my best to avoid the gangs. Occasionally, I ran into my buddies. One of our favorite pastimes was to hang around the train station, waiting for the shopkeeper to throw out expired candy. We would pick through the pile after the shopkeeper left, sniffing and examining the candy to make sure it was not rotten before popping it into our mouths. Those were good times.

But mostly I was alone. I was alone, yet there were always people around. Living on the streets meant I never had any privacy—but I'd never had any privacy at the orphanage, either. I passed people on the streets all the time, and there were people who saw me every day—shopkeepers, stall holders, street vendors, people on their way to work, kids going to and from school—but I never paid much attention to them because they never paid any attention to me.

To an outsider, the life of a street child is beyond comprehension. Perhaps that was why we were overlooked, ignored, and treated like we were not even there.

If anyone *had* noticed me on the street, my face simply would have blurred into all the other faces of the countless street children who roamed the streets of Manila. I was just another faceless orphan, a street kid left in the streets of Manila to fend for myself and to make my way in the world.

Manila was a city overflowing with poverty, with shantytowns sprawled across the urban landscape. With so many people living in tiny, rough-hewn houses made of tin, used, rotted plywood and cardboard that were stacked precariously on top of one another and crowded side by side, no one noticed one more kid in the street. No one asked where my mommy was or why I was not in school.

And so I walked alone night after night, orphaned and alone, wheeling along my precious cargo of trash.

I pushed my cart to the front of the junk shop and waited as Jack weighed the contents. I had worked solo that night, so it had been a lot of work, and I had few rare items, including a solid copper pipe. I thought it was a good night, and I was tired.

"You get thirty pesos tonight," Jack said and handed me the money. "Good job!"

Thirty pesos! I hit the jackpot! I'd never had that much money in my hands at one time. Thirty pesos was much more than what I usually made. I was proud of myself. I was so excited that my tiredness vanished. I did not want to go to sleep right away, even though the sun was already up and the streets were coming alive with activity.

The money was burning a hole in my hands. *What should I do with it?* My mind was reeling a mile a minute. I sat on a curb and contemplated my options, my thoughts bouncing from candy to toys to a nice, hot chicken leg. Then it dawned on me. *I know—I'll buy some new clothes!* I thought excitedly. My shirt was dirty and full of holes, and my shorts were stained and tearing in a few different places. These were the same clothes I had worn at the orphanage, and they were starting to get really ratty because of my new job. I was barefoot because I had outgrown and outworn my last pair of shoes at Kabataan. The thought of all-new clothes, including new sandals, was overwhelming. I was nearly dizzy with joy.

As soon as the nearest shop opened, I went in and selected new shorts, a new shirt, and new sandals. I held them in my hands for a long time, admiring the crisp feel and clean scent of the fabric. It was so exciting to have new clothes, especially ones that I bought with my own money.

Just as I was about to put them on, I realized that if I wore them, they would just get as dirty as my old clothes. A wave of sadness swept over me.

What should I do? I wondered. *I can't wear these. They're too nice.* After a few moments, I had an idea. *I'll hide them somewhere safe so that when I see Mom and Dad again, I can have nice new clothes to wear. I can show them how good and smart I am. They'll be really pleased that I made it on my own!*

With this new plan, I was once again excited about my new clothes. I would save them for that one special day. I carefully wrapped my new clothes back in the plastic bag and hid the parcel in a secret spot under the bridge. As the sun rose, I went to sleep with a satisfied smile on his face.

That evening, I awoke in a celebratory mood. I still had some money left over. I found Joe and Sonny and told them about my good fortune from the night before.

"Good job, Butch!" Sonny slapped me on the back.

"Well done!" Joe said. "You know what this means—we have to celebrate!"

"Yeah, let's celebrate!" I beamed, happy with the attention and camaraderie. "How should we celebrate?" I asked. I was not used to celebrating anything.

"I know just the thing," Joe said with a wink. He led us to a nearby shop. Blues music wafted through the air from a nearby jukebox. "Give me your money and wait here—I'll be right back."

Joe entered into the shop and emerged a few minutes later with a bottle of clear liquid and handed it to me.

"What's this?" I eyed the bottle.

"It's gin!" Joe said. "You've never had gin?"

"No," I said. I did not even know what gin was. "Is it good?"

"Oh, yeah!" Joe said, grinning. "Come on, let's go sit on the bridge and celebrate!"

As soon as the first drop of gin reached my tongue, I recoiled and made a face. It burned my throat, and I spat most of it out, surprised by its bad taste. I did not understand why Joe thought this awful drink would be good for a celebration. But everyone else seemed to like it, so I kept drinking. I swallowed quickly to minimize the awful taste. I had no idea what it would do to me. I thought it was simply a nasty-tasting drink, but the more I drank, the better it tasted.

Before long, we were all roaring with laughter as the night grew darker and the moon grew bigger. Everything was hilarious. I wondered why my speech was slurred, and I laughed at my inability to speak coherently. I did not have a care in the world! At eleven years old, I was drunk for the first time. More than that, though, I felt that I was a part of something, part of a gang of boys who shared my misery and perhaps even my loneliness.

After a couple of hours, the bottle of gin was completely empty—and so was my stomach. I had not had anything to eat since I had woken up, and I was starting to feel nauseated. My mind was spinning, and my eyes could not focus. The next thing I knew, I was doubled over the edge of the bridge, throwing up into the river below—the same black river where the sewer emptied, where boys excreted their own waste, and where people dumped their garbage. I had no idea what was going on or why I was sick, but everyone was laughing at me, so something must have been funny.

A few hours later, I woke up with a massive headache. Groaning, I held my head and looked around. Somehow I had wound up in the cart with Joe fast asleep on top of me. I was naked. I did not want to think about what might have been done to me. I did not think this sexual exploitation would happen in the streets as it had in the orphanage. I ignored the thoughts. I must have passed out, but I did not remember anything, and I did not want to remember anything. My body ached, my stomach hurt, and my mind still reeled. Slowly I shoved Joe off of me, sat up, and held my head. After a few moments, I hobbled off the cart.

I felt horrible all day, physically and emotionally. As my aches slowly eased, I remembered the events of the day before. *I bought new clothes!* I thought with sudden clarity.

I went back to the secluded spot under the bridge, eager to see my new clothes. I reached my hand into the secret nook where I had stealthily hidden my prized possessions, but nothing was there. I searched desperately all around the bridge but could not find anything. My new clothes were gone. I collapsed to the ground and cried. This day would forever define how I looked at life and money. If things change so rapidly, I would live each day as if it were the last.

I learned several lessons that day: I never again drank gin, and I never again bought anything new to set aside and not use right away. And I could never again trust that anyone was truly my friend.

Life on the streets was not easy, but neither was life in Kabataan. Every day I tried to decide which place was better, but I never came to any conclusions. Both were terrible. Even so, I somehow liked living on the streets better because at least I had freedom. I did not have to worry about restrictive house parents dictating everything or other kids beating me up.

For the first few months I lived on the streets, I did not think about my brothers that often. I did not have time; life was too much about survival. I had my own troubles and concerns now. Adriano and Bobby would just have to look out for themselves.

A lot of kids were living like me on the streets—many more than the small group I hung out with. For the most part, the different groups of kids left each other alone. They stayed on their own turf. There was an unspoken rule among the street kids that if you got to a pile of garbage and a cart was already there, you left that pile alone until the kid who got there first was finished. It was like an honor system, a way of keeping things civilized.

One night, I was pushing the cart alone when four kids I did not know ran up and started taking stuff off of my cart.

"Hey! What are you doing?" I shouted.

Boom! One of the kids knocked me to the ground. My legs shook as I stood up, but there was nothing I could do—there were four of them and only one of me. If I tried to fight, I would be beaten to a pulp. I raced back to my home base.

"Joe! Sonny! Come quick, some kids just hit me, and they're stealing stuff off my cart!"

I rounded up a few kids, and together we ran back to my cart. The rival gang was still there, but on the other side of the street. Joe lifted a rock and pelted it at one of the boys. There was a cry of surprise, followed by a series of curses, and then it was war.

Rocks were hurled back and forth across the street as obscenities erupted from our lips. I threw anything I could find—garbage, metal, rocks, anything and everything! There seemed to be an equal number of kids on both sides of the fight, but the other kids were not tough enough. Eventually the intruders backed down and went back across the river. We cheered and shouted at the other kids never to come back to our side of town again, or else. I had fresh stains on my shirt and could taste blood on my lip, but it was the bittersweet taste of revenge. Sonny and I slapped each other on the back and crossed the street to retrieve the cart.

It was good to have buddies like Sonny, Joe, and the other kids we worked with. It was like having some sort of protection. I could depend on them when the going got too rough, which happened plenty of times. This was not the first street fight I had gotten into. There were times when other kids had thrown stones at me while I was working my route. Every time it happened, I fled straight to home base and gathered the troops. They were more than happy to stick up for one another. That's how gangs were formed; a single kid by himself could never make it alone on the streets.

Even though I had the protection and companionship of some of the street kids, day after day I woke up on my cardboard box alone and wandered the streets by myself. It was a desolate existence. Everyone I passed on the street stared past me as if I did not exist, and some days I began to wonder if I even existed at all.

My Third Parents

One lonely night, several months after running away from Kabataan, I found myself sitting on the bridge gazing up at the beautiful sky with the stars spread before me, sprinkled against the darkness. The city was quiet. The night was peaceful.

My thoughts strayed back to my brothers, still helpless and alone at Kabataan. I worried about them, but I knew they were mostly OK because they were not on the streets like I was. I loved my brothers more than anything in the world, and it pained me that we could not be together.

On nights like those, I yearned for companionship. I wished my brothers were there with me on the bridge to look up at the sky and enjoy God's amazing work. I also wished my mom was there to hold me, but I did not know why. I could not explain why I still longed for the person who abandoned me, who left me and my brothers without looking back.

On countless nights, I prayed to God to reunite me with my mother. I begged, pleaded, and bargained with God, but nothing worked. I asked God why He took away my mother…I never received any answers.

Perhaps the one redeeming feature of growing up in the orphanages was that they taught us Roman Catholic values. They taught us to believe that God was always listening, so He would always hear our prayers. They taught us right from wrong, and I was always very clear about doing the right thing because I believed that God was not just listening; He was watching, too.

Even when I could barely walk from the sharp hunger pangs stabbing my stomach, I had never considered stealing food. I always headed for the nearest trash pile instead.

One night, I was not able to find anything edible in the trash. I looked in all the usual spots—behind restaurants, near rich people's homes, next to street vendors—but there was not anything edible anywhere. I was hungry. It was not trash night, so I was not going to make much money that night, if at all.

Between 3:00 and 4:00 a.m., the fruit and vegetable vendors began to set up their stalls in the street. Usually I passed them by without a second thought, but this time my hunger was too strong. I stood at the side of the street and watched them from a distance, uneasy about what I planned to do. It was too early for customers, so the vendors often dozed before the customers arrived. After setting up his stand, one of the vendors fell sound asleep next to his cart of vegetables. I seized the opportunity. I crept up to the vegetable stand and snatched a huge pineapple, darting away down the street before anyone would notice.

I ran down the street, breathing heavily. *I've just stolen this pineapple*, I thought. *I just took something that isn't mine. I took this without paying for it.* These thoughts whirled mercilessly through my mind. I slowed to a walk. I looked at the pineapple and thought about my crime while my stomach grumbled. It was a crime, and worse—it was a crime against God.... *It was a sin.*

Staring down at the pineapple, I was flooded with guilt. I wanted to sneak back and return it to the vendor, but I was afraid that if the vendor found out, I would get whipped—or worse, be arrested and sent away to some place even worse than Kabataan.

I made my way back to home base, where Sonny, Joe, and a few other kids were hanging out after working all night.

"Hey, I found this in the trash," I said, handing them the pineapple. "I'm not hungry—you guys eat it."

Without another word, I turned and walked away. With my stomach aching so much, I could not bear to watch my friends eat the pineapple. I continued roaming the streets, looking for piles of garbage where I might find something I could eat.

Every now and then, I had some extra cash. Because there was no point in buying new clothes or anything nice, I decided to learn how to ride a bike.

I'd gotten the idea a few days earlier, after several street kids nearly ran me over as they whizzed by on bicycles.

How did they get bikes? I had wondered as I watched them race back and forth. I knew they could not possibly have bought them.

Following at a safe distance, I watched them ride up and down the streets, doing pop-a-wheelies and other tricks. After a while, the kids pedaled to a storefront, where they hopped off the bikes and wheeled them inside. The sign out front read "Bikes for Rent." I had never ridden a bike before, but I was determined to try it the next time I made enough money to spare.

After a successful night of work, I slept for a few hours, then awoke in the afternoon. I ate a small meal, then excitedly raced over to the bike rental shop.

"I'd like to rent a bike, sir," I said to the shopkeeper.

The shopkeeper eyed me with suspicion, "You have the money?"

"Yes," I said, handing him a fistful of change.

"OK," the shopkeeper said after counting it. "We'll let you ride you this small bike here. Bring it back by five p.m."

I gently wheeled a small, beat-up bike out of the shop, full of great fascination for this temporary treasure. I quickly wheeled the bike to an empty alley and hopped on. This was going to be fun!

Gently propping myself up on the seat, I teetered back and forth on my feet, trying to find my balance. My toes could barely touch the ground. The bike felt so wobbly. With a deep breath, I lifted my feet and pushed myself forward. I rolled a few feet before falling over with a heavy crash. Unsure what I had done wrong, I got on the bike again, steadied myself, and began peddling furiously. Within seconds, I crashed into a pile of boxes, sending garbage scattering everywhere.

The other kids made it look so easy, but riding a bike was actually proving to be tricky. I picked myself up and got on the bike again. And again, and again. Soon both knees were scraped and bloody, but the frustration just made me more determined.

It was not long before a group of street kids gathered to watch, laughing and egging me on. I was used to being laughed at, picked on, and teased, so I just gritted my teeth, ignored them the best I could, and got on the bike again.

I spent hours wobbling and wiggling all over the street on that bike, riding a few feet and then falling off and picking myself up again. Once I managed to go forward more than a few feet, I would get so excited that I would forget to steer, and I would crash head first into something or else twist the bike so far around that I just fell over. Once I got the hang of steering, I would forget to pedal, and then the bike would fall over because it lost momentum. It was momentous victory when I figured out (at last) how to peddle *and* steer *and* stay balanced in a straight line! However, I did not know how to brake because I had not yet gotten to the point where I needed the brakes—so I crashed.

By the end of the day, after several exhausting and frustrating hours wobbling on the street and lying on the ground with the bike twisted on top of me, all of the elements miraculously came together. It was scary at first because I knew I could crash or fall over again at any minute, but once I got the hang of it, I just kept riding, sailing through the city on my bike with the wind in my face and the pavement underneath my wheels. It was exhilarating!

When 5:00 p.m. rolled around, I wheeled the bike back to the shop, immensely proud of my achievement. I was glad that the bike was already beat up because the owner would not notice all the new dents and scratches it now had. I certainly got my money's worth with that bike.

As I walked away from the bike shop, a satisfied and triumphant smile spread across my face. I had relished all those frustrating hours on the bike because simply having a bike in the first place made me feel important, as if I *had* something. Once I had learned to ride, it was pure enjoyment. This was the first time I truly made the connection between hard work and enjoying the fruits of my labor. I learned that if I made enough money, I could get something and enjoy it.

My Third Parents

A few days after mastering the bike, I had another successful night of work. Instead of treating myself to another bike ride, I went to the candy shop and stocked up on a pocketful of Sampalok, a tamarind candy coated with sugar. I also loaded up on other powdered candies made from sugared flour. After eating several pieces, I asked Sonny to show me the way back to the orphanage. I offered him a few pieces of candy in exchange for the favor.

"You can find your way back?" Sonny asked after we reached the orphanage. I nodded.

"OK, good. I am not sticking around. Be careful—if the house parents see you, they will snatch you up and force you back into the orphanage!"

I shuddered at the thought, thanked my friend, then nimbly slipped through the small hole in the fence behind Cottage 6.

On the other side of the fence, I stood very still and quietly looked around. I did not want too many people to see me. It had been a long time since I had been at the orphanage, and I was overwhelmed with a range of emotions. I was immensely relieved that I did not live there anymore. Just being there made my chest tighten as the memories came flooding back. I tried to shake them from my mind. I wanted to find my brothers as soon as possible and then get out of there.

After a few minutes, some kids walked by.

"Psst!" I whispered. "Hey, you!"

The kids looked around and saw me partially hidden in the bushes. Curious, they walked over. When they recognized me, they fired off a thousand questions, but I did not have the patience to answer them.

"Hey, I don't have much time. Go get Adriano and Bobby; I need to talk to them! Don't tell anyone else that I'm here."

The kids ran off. I prayed that they would not tell the house parents I was there. I also kept an eye out for bullies or other kids who might tell on me. Although it was only a few minutes, it felt like an eternity before Adriano and Bobby arrived.

"Butch!" they cried and threw their arms around me. "Where were you? Where have you been?" They were so happy to see me again.

"I've been living on the streets, working and looking for Mom and Dad," I explained. "Are you OK?"

"Yeah, we're OK. We go to the gate every day waiting for you to come back," Adriano said. "We do that every day. We've been waiting a long time!"

I felt a pang of guilt at those words because I knew how it felt to walk to the gate every day, waiting in vain for someone to show up. I knew the enormous sense of loss they both must have felt when I disappeared.

"Hey, I brought you this," I said, putting a pile of candies into each of their hands.

"Wow!" Bobby said, excited. They beamed at me.

"Eat it now or hide it," I instructed. "Listen, I gotta go, but I'll come back later with more candy."

"OK," they said. I knew they were sad to see me go, but I hoped they were also happy to know that I was OK and that I cared enough to come back and see them.

"Take care of yourselves," I said and quickly slipped back through the hole in the fence.

Back on the streets alone again, I moped, my eyes sweeping back and forth on the ground as I walked. The most important lesson I learned from finding value in other people's waste was that it was possible to find things anywhere, at any time. With every step, I stared fixedly at the ground in case I found something valuable, edible, or recyclable. Wherever I went, I was always looking down for the entire walk. I rarely saw the sky because there was nothing up there that could help me. I felt that even God was not there for me anymore.

Weeks and months passed. I had no concept of time, and I did not need to. At some point, I was pretty sure I must have had a birthday. I did not have a calendar, so I could not be sure, but I thought I turned twelve years old.

I did not tell anybody because there was no point. There was nothing to celebrate. Besides, I did not want to get drunk again.

Each day was the same—working from roughly 10:00 p.m. until 4:00 a.m. and then sleeping until the early afternoon. There was nowhere I had to be and no schedule I needed to follow other than to work extra hard on garbage nights. As a street kid, I was always on the job. There was no telling when I might run across something useful or valuable. I was a hard worker because my life was at stake. To slack off or take a night off from work meant I would not have anything to eat.

Kids came and went on the streets. Sonny disappeared after a while. I had no idea where he went, and neither did anyone else. It was just part of street life—I had no one to rely on but myself. I had to take everything as it came (and went), from food to friendship.

As bad as things were on the streets, I never succumbed to thievery, violence, drugs, or alcoholism. The kids who were sniffing glue always asked me to join them, but I just wasn't interested. I never got into drinking like the other kids did, either. Because of all the shady things going on in the streets, I kept to myself.

There were so many kids living on the streets that I wondered where they all came from. Some of them were abused, some were abandoned, some had been kicked out of their homes. Some of them had homes, but for one reason or another, being on the streets was actually better than living with their families. Every one of them had a story that led up to their lives on the streets, but none of them really talked about it much. Perhaps it was too depressing.

I never stopped praying to God to help him me of my hopeless situation, although my faith wavered. I often felt that even God had abandoned me. I pleaded with God, "If you give me a chance, dear Lord, I will help these kids who need help. I will help the children in the orphanage, too. I want all of us to have a chance at a better life."

One day after a long night picking up garbage, I woke up around noon with the sun shining directly above me, beating against my face. I lifted my hand to cover my eyes when suddenly a shadow eclipsed the brightness and a face came into view, hovering above me.

"Hi," a female voice said. "I'm Mrs. Gonzales." She peered down at me. "I have a farm, and I need some help. Do you want to come and work on my farm?"

I sat up immediately and got a better look at her. She was in her midthirties, and she was alone. She knelt down beside me.

"I have a place at my farm where you can sleep," the woman continued. "I can give you food if you help watch our ducks. And if you help with planting rice, you can make some money."

She seemed to be a nice woman. She was very kind and spoke softly.

"Yes, OK, I'll go with you," I said right away. "I'll work on your farm."

I had never worked on a farm before, but it sounded a lot better than living on the streets. Besides, I had nothing to lose.

"How did you know to ask me?" I asked her, curiously.

She pointed to a little stand nearby that was selling homemade food. "They recommended you," she said. "They said that you were a good worker, that you were honest and trustworthy." She smiled. "Can you come with me today?"

"Yes, I can go right now," I said, standing up.

"Excellent. Do you need to gather your things?" she asked.

"No," I shook my head. "I don't have anything."

Chapter 5

The Farm

A loud whistle pierced the air as a shout echoed along the platform. "All aboard!" repeated the old, fat conductor several times before hopping on the train.

I sat across from Mrs. Gonzales and looked around the compartment. I was fascinated by its structure and wondered how long it took to build this train. As we pulled away from the station, I watched as the trees and telephone poles began to move slowly by and then sped to in a rapid blur. I was struck with apprehension at my split-second decision to join this woman and go with her to work on her farm. Had I made the right choice? Would I ever see my brothers again? Worried thoughts tumbled through my twelve-year-old mind.

"You ever been in the train?" a boy next to me asked. I was so consumed with paranoia and worry that I did not even hear the little boy speaking. The boy tapped my shoulder ever so lightly, causing me to jump and nearly fall out of my seat.

"You ever been in the train?" the boy repeated patiently.

I shook my head and watched the blurred landscape zooming past. Clenching my jaws and fists, I tried not to cry. My eyes were tearing up, and I blinked and blinked. No one would understand. Anger and frustration about my life situation surged through my veins. I wanted to cry, but my sense of manhood forced me to fight back the tears, despite the enormous pain I felt. The rhythm of the train eventually hushed my troubled thoughts and lulled me to sleep.

More than five hours later, Mrs. Gonzales stood and announced, "We're here!" I woke up from a dreamless sleep. I followed Mrs. Gonzales off the train and stepped into a strange new world.

The earth was blanketed in darkness. The city lights were nowhere to be found; we really were out in the country now. Off in the distance, a tiny light flickered.

"That's our house," Mrs. Gonzales said, pointing. "And this is the farm where you're going to be working." She swept her arm to indicate the space in front of us. As my eyes adjusted, I could begin to see the rice fields and make out the distant shape of the house about a quarter of a mile away. I wondered how we were going to get there.

"You sure don't talk much," Mrs. Gonzales remarked, not expecting an answer.

"Hi, Mom!" I was startled by the voice that suddenly rang out of nowhere. A nine-year-old boy darted out from the darkness to greet us.

"Hi, Sam," Mrs. Gonzales said, reaching out her arm and giving the boy a hug. "I would like you to meet Butch. He will be working for us."

"Hi, Butch."

"Hi," I said quietly.

The little boy led us back to the house, with his mom following right behind him. I watched them carefully as my eyes struggled to adjust to the pitch-black darkness. I could barely discern a narrow path made of raised mud lining the edge of the rice field. The path was only a foot wide. The fields on either side appeared to be filled with water.

The little boy raced across the path like a practiced gymnast on a balance beam. I tentatively stepped onto the moonlit path, concentrating on every stride, looking down at my feet to make sure they were still on the path.

"Butch, come on!" Sam shouted. I looked up briefly as I carefully found my way along the dark path, and then there was a *splash* as I struck the muddy earth and black water flew into the air. I struggled to pull myself up from the rice paddy, my body and face covered with thick muck. I was soaked.

My Third Parents

Sam laughed and shouted, "You'll get used to it," looking backward at me as he continued to run forward. Sam could run without even looking and not lose his balance.

When we reached the house, Mrs. Gonzales told me to wait outside. She returned moments later with clean clothes and instructed me to change out of my muddy clothes before entering the house.

"Would you like some dinner?" she asked after I had changed into the clean clothes.

I nodded silently.

She showed me into the wooden house, where the family sat at a candlelit table. The house did not have electricity, so the room was lit with an eerie, flickering glow that cast an orange light on their faces. I was introduced to Mr. Gonzales, and I could tell that he was used to working in the rice fields because his skin was very dark from constant sun exposure. He was an interesting-looking man, very tall and skinny, with a sunken chin and a prominent jaw. He did not speak much; Mrs. Gonzales did all of the talking.

"You've already met Sam, and these are our daughters, Alice and Kate," she said. Alice was the youngest, probably around seven years old, and Kate was a bit older than me. They said hi, but other than that they did not talk to me that much—they were too busy trying to tell their mom about what happened in school that day. I was fine with being ignored; I was too overwhelmed at this sudden change of scenery. Simply sitting down to dinner with a family caused a torrent of mixed emotions to race through me with alarming intensity. It had been an unbelievably long time since I had last sat down to a family dinner, and even though the family was not my own, it felt alluring and incredibly uncomfortable at the same time. I was not used to it.

Their house seemed huge, but I was not allowed to sleep there. I was told that I was allowed in the house only at meal times. After dinner, Mrs. Gonzales showed me my hut. It was basically an outdoor structure next to their house with bamboo walls and a bamboo floor. The roof was made out of coconut tree leaves fashioned into a triangular shape at the top.

"We'll explain your chores to you in the morning," Mrs. Gonzales said before wishing me a good night.

She did not give me a blanket or a pillow, so I lay down on the hard bamboo floor. Through the walls, I could hear the frogs ribbiting, crickets chirping, and various other sounds of the night. It was just like sleeping outside.

It was not luxurious, but it was my own place. My own private, personal place. I immediately liked it much better than sleeping on the streets. I did not have to worry about anyone stepping on me or kids running me over with their bikes. I did not have to worry about shop owners telling me to get up and move along. The night was peaceful.

I drifted off to sleep. A few hours later I awoke, but I was not even sure I was awake because everything was shrouded in darkness. I could not even see my hand in front of my face. It was almost scary because I had gotten used to sleeping under the blazing sun and roaming at night under the dim streetlights.

I wondered how my brothers back at Kabataan were doing. After a silent, tearful prayer asking God to take care of them, I fell back asleep until morning.

Morning dew covered the ground. As the frogs fell silent, the birds began their mating calls, bathed in the rising sunlight. It was too early to begin my chores, but the sharp cry of the roosters urged me out of slumber. I emerged from my bamboo hut, scanning my new surroundings for the first time in the golden dawn.

Endless rice fields stretched out before me, divided into squares by narrow paths like the one I had taken the night before. The paddies were filled with water two feet deep, in preparation for planting. Trees dotted the horizon and between them, I could see the shapes of various wooden structures. Everywhere I looked, I saw the lush green of the countryside. Not a single person was in sight, which was a shock after living on the city streets. Even though it was peaceful and beautiful, I felt scared about being in such unfamiliar surroundings and once again prayed that I had made the right choice.

I studied the Gonzales house, seeing it for the first time in the light. It was a weathered wooden structure, but it was still standing and appeared solid—unlike many of the houses in Manila's shantytowns. I thought it was a nice house.

I looked in the direction we had walked the previous night, shuddering as I remembered tumbling into the muck. I strained to see the place where the train had let us off, but there was nothing there now. My brothers back at Kabataan now felt so far away. I fought back tears.

I was gazing at the sodden rice paddies, quietly absorbing the beauty of the rural sunrise, when Mrs. Gonzales stepped out of the house.

"You're up early!" she exclaimed. "Good. Let me show you what to do."

She led me to the back of the house where they kept a chicken coop and showed me how to feed the chickens. She demonstrated how to carefully take the chicken and duck eggs from the hay and place them in a basket. This was an important task because every morning she took the basketful of eggs to sell at the market. Duck eggs are a delicacy in the Philippines, called *balut*. People boiled the eggs with the nearly developed embryos still inside, which would be eaten inside the shell.

After feeding the chickens and collecting the eggs, my next task for the rest of the day was to tend to the flock of thirty or forty ducks. By then, Mr. Gonzales returned from the rice fields and explained what I had to do as his wife left for the market. My job was to walk the ducks to the river so that they could eat and to keep an eye on them so that they would not get stolen by neighboring farmers, eaten by snakes, or lured away by wild ducks. Mr. Gonzales explained that even though the ducks had their wings clipped and could not fly away, they had a tendency to follow the wild geese because they were once wild themselves.

"Be sure to always carry one of these," Mr. Gonzales said, handing me a machete. "You will need this to protect the ducks from the hungry reptiles."

I gulped, yet I remained poised and tried to show no sign of fear. "Yes sir."

Mr. Gonzales left. I turned to face the ducks, who were all quacking and nipping at the ground. "It's just you and me now," I said to them.

"That way, go that way!" I yelled, running behind the ducks. I ran to the left of them and to the right of them, trying to get them to waddle over to the river. "No, no, do not go in the field! Go to the river!" I ordered, but the ducks quacked and paid no attention.

I stopped and sighed. Collecting the ducks' eggs was an easy task, but getting these birds in the river was exhausting. My voice got hoarse from yelling. The ducks would not do what I said. How would I get them to the river?

After much effort, I finally persuaded them to march in the right direction. Once they were swimming around in the water, I idly picked up a rock and threw it in the river to vent my frustration. "Finally!" I yelled at the ducks. They quickly swam away from the loud splash. "That's interesting," I thought. I threw another rock. The ducks once again swam away from it, quacking furiously. Delighted with this new discovery, I continually threw rocks behind the herd to make them move forward. After about a quarter mile of pitching, they finally reached a feasible feeding area.

The blinding sun of the afternoon heat burned into my skin, making me drowsy. I sought shade under the protective leaves of a short banana tree, where I could keep a close eye on the ducks and watch out for wild geese and reptiles.

Two hours later, the heat was unbearable. My dry throat burned with thirst. After watching the ducks swimming contentedly in the river, I threw off my clothes and dove in. The water was amazingly clear and refreshing, instantly soothing my hot skin and quenching my parched throat. With my eyes wide open, I floated underwater and watched the bubbles ascend to the surface. To my right, I could see dozens of webbed feet wiggling back and forth. I got an idea.

I resurfaced and quickly took a large breath before diving back under the water, paddling slowly and quietly. I stealthily swam underneath a duck, grabbed its feet and yanked it to the bottom. What fun! As the duck squawked, kicked, and struggled for breath, the others panicked and swam for safety. I laughed and screamed with delight at the mayhem I had caused.

Still laughing at my little joke, I got up out of the river so that I could regroup the herd. As I started to slip on my shorts, I noticed a black, slick piece of slime stuck between my legs. I attempted to flick it off with my finger but could not. My skin puckered as I struggled to pluck it off. Then, finally, it snapped off. Blood dripped from my leg.

"That was gross," I thought. Almost as an afterthought, I decided to look myself over. To my horror, I discovered that more of the slimy black things were stuck to my arms and shoulder. With a shout, I quickly yanked off the leeches, throwing them to the ground. With the machete, I hacked them quickly into little pieces and buried them under my feet so that they would not be able to come back to life and jump on me.

"Quack," came from the direction of the river. "Quack, quack."

"You think that's funny, huh?" I said to the ducks who were watching me.

By then the sun had begun its descent, and a cool breeze was wafting through the countryside. The hungry herd had been screaming for the last hour. I realized that it was probably about time for them to be fed the unhusked rice that Mr. Gonzales had shown me earlier. I struggled to herd them back to the farm for their evening feeding.

After feeding the ducks, I waited to be called in to dinner. I ate with the family once more, but I stayed very quiet as they all chatted about their day, feeling out of place there. I was both happy and uncomfortable. I was happy because for the first time in a long, long time, I had enough to eat. I would not go to bed hungry and best of all, I did not have to eat half-rotten food from the garbage. Yet I was uncomfortable because I did not know these people. I felt several steps below the children of the family because they went to school while I had to work and because they had kind parents who were taking care of them, while I was nothing but an abandoned orphan. As the family chattered around me, I longed for my brothers and wondered how they were doing.

That night, I lay alone in my little hut, listening to the croaking frogs, and cried myself to sleep.

After two months at my new job, I discovered that the ducks had become conditioned to respond to my call. Every time I created a clamor with my tin bucket, which I usually used to pour the grain out of, the herd trampled hurriedly and hungrily toward me. It was a great way to control their movements.

Now, instead of yelling myself hoarse whenever I wanted to organize the herd to go somewhere, I simply clanged the tin can. Every day, I herded the ducks to the river to eat the fish that moved quickly through the clear water, and then at the end of the day I returned them to the farm.

For the most part, it was boring work, but I was not complaining. At least it was work, and it was better than picking through garbage all night. I spent all day alone with the ducks, so I had to find ways to entertain myself. Sometimes I swam in the water; other times I dozed under the trees with my machete at my side. Most days were uneventful.

However, on one occasion, I noticed a break on the water's otherwise smooth surface. A duck suddenly disappeared underneath the water. Puzzled, I stepped closer to the bank and peered into the river, waiting for the missing duck to resurface. As I gazed into the now-silent river, a seven-foot-long yellow snake slithered silently across my feet. Startled, I jumped back and hurriedly drew my short bolo machete, which I'd never had to use before, out of its wooden sheath.

The snake swiftly slithered into a deep hole in the ground and disappeared. With my heart hammering in my chest, I debated what to do. It was my job to watch the ducks and prevent the snakes from eating them, after all. Would I get in trouble for the missing duck? Would they kick me back out onto the streets?

I tiptoed over to the large, dark hole. Using the machete, I tried to dig the snake out of the hole, but I was terrified. The snake was gigantic, and I feared it could swallow me whole.

Without another thought, I ran back to the farm, clutching my machete for protection.

"Mr. Gonzales, Mr. Gonzales!" I shouted frantically when I reached the farmhouse.

"What is it?" Mr. Gonzales asked, running over from the rice field.

"A snake, there's a giant snake that just ate a duck!" I said in a rush. "I tried to kill it, but it went underground."

"Show me where the snake is."

The two of us raced back to the river where the other ducks were swimming and quacking as if nothing unusual had happened. I pointed out the snake hole to Mr. Gonzales.

"It's in there," I said.

Mr. Gonzales did not waste a single moment. He expertly dug his machete into the hole and showed me how to help him dig. We dug really deep before we saw the snake. Mr. Gonzales forced the writhing snake out of the hole and immediately hacked it with his machete. I watched in awe and horror, my own machete lying limp at my side, until Mr. Gonzales said, "Help me chop it up, quick!" I lifted my machete and brought it down on the huge, scaly beast. Blood poured from the wounds. In its belly, the snake still had a huge bump from where it had swallowed the duck. I was scared. The snake was so big that it could easily have been *me* in its belly instead of the duck.

With a few expert motions, Mr. Gonzales managed to chop off the snake's head. Finally the snake was dead. At that moment, I realized that my job watching the ducks may not be so easy after all; unseen dangers lurked in hidden places. Weary from the day's commotion, I walked the rest of the ducks back to the farm and put them away for the night.

Later, I lay alone in my little hut, staring at the early moon while the Gonzales family rested quietly in the house. My thoughts drifted to my brothers. I never went to sleep without mourning for them. My hunger was not for food anymore, but for them. Although my physical hunger was now satiated, my loneliness never eased.

Dear God, I prayed silently. *Can you please tell my mother and my father where I am so that they can come get me? Can you please watch over Adriano and Bobby until I can go back and get them?*

Tears ran silently down my face as sleep overcame me.

"Planting rice is never fun, bent from dawn 'til the setting sun. Cannot stand and cannot sit, cannot rest for a little bit…." The words of the Filipino folk song echoed through the fields.

It was planting season. I had a new job at the farm, this time working in the rice paddies from dawn until dusk. To plant the rice, I was constantly bent over at the waist as I tramped slowly through the wet fields carrying a bag of fresh, young rice shoots. One at a time, I pulled out small clusters from the bag and embedded them into the sodden earth a few inches apart. It was an enormous amount of work, going row by row until all of the rice paddies were filled with thin, grassy stalks. I paused to rest for a few short seconds in muddy water nearly up to my knees. I looked up to watch the soaring birds, my back aching as I slowly straightened myself. Planting rice was nowhere near as fun as riding the water buffalo had been.

Before we'd begun planting the rice, we'd plowed the fields with the help of a water buffalo called a "carabao." I had ridden on the back of the large, fat animal while it dragged a plow behind it to break up the soil. Even though it was technically work, riding the carabao had been fun.

One day, I was riding the back of the male carabao when suddenly it bucked me off and tore across the fields toward a female carabao, which must have been in heat. I sank deep into the soft mud while everyone nearly fell over laughing because I couldn't control the giant beast. Several farmers ran to catch the carabao before it broke up too much of the rice fields.

After we finished plowing the field each day, we took the carabao to the river to wash off the muck. That was also fun because I got to swim with the giant, gentle beast, who loved being in the water as much as I did.

Now that the plowing was finished, I slaved in the rice fields with the other workers. Planting rice was much harder physical labor than riding the carabao or watching the ducks, so I went to bed aching and sore at the end of each day.

In my little hut, I tried to calculate how much time had passed since I last saw my brothers. I had lost track, but it had been too long. I was ready to see them again. I worried most about Bobby and prayed that the bullies were not sexually abusing and humiliating him or beating him up for his food. I prayed that Bobby was getting enough to eat. I felt so helpless, lying there all alone, unable to do more than pray, so far away from my brothers. I prayed that someday things would get better.

Eventually, it was harvest time (this was somewhere in June; we had planted the rice in February). The paddies that had once been full of mud had transformed into fields brimming with tall, green leaves. When the rice was tall and brown at the top, it was ready to be pulled from the ground. Many different birds flocked in the field and soared through the sky, hoping to get some of the rice. The farmers stalked the area with their nets and their BB guns, while the children crept around with their slings. When they were successful, the bird became their dinner.

Harvesting the rice was a family effort—even the farmer's children took part, along with a bunch of people I had never seen before. They showed me how to grab a bunch of rice plants with one hand and then whack at it with a sickle just above the roots. The green rice plant would then be thrown into a pile as we continued cutting the field.

The farmer explained that the rice would be put into sacks and sold according to weight. He promised that I would be paid for half of what I harvested. With this motivation, I worked in the fields from dawn 'til dusk harvesting rice, even though my thighs were killing me, my calves were sore, and my back and arms ached. I worked with my hands all day, without sitting down or standing straight, until the field was cleared. It took me two days.

I harvested three huge sacks of rice, which I then had to cut and husk manually. I pushed the unhusked rice into a pile and then beat it to pop the kernels out of the leaves. I filtered out the debris by putting the rice into a pan and tossing it into the air, allowing the wind to blow away the empty husks while the kernels remained in the pan. I poured the remaining rice into a sack that the farmer weighed. I earned twenty-five pesos for each bushel, reaping seventy-five pesos for my hard work.

Knowing that the harvest season was at its end and I had collected enough money, I knew it was time to return to see my brothers. Having made that decision, I went to Mrs. Gonzales at the end of the day and said to her, "I would like to return to Manila to visit my brothers."

"OK," she said without argument. "You have enough money to buy a train ticket back to Manila, and you will have some left over. There is a train this evening—if you hurry, you can catch it now before it leaves. You've been a good worker, Butch."

I thanked Mrs. Gonzales and her husband and said good-bye to their children. I was grateful to this family for helping me in many ways; they had sheltered me, taken me off the streets, and given me a time of peace at the farm. I hoped that someday I would have a family as nice as they were, with a mom, dad, brothers, and sisters all together. After waving good-bye, I ran swiftly across the narrow pathway through the rice paddies, without looking down even once, and boarded the train bound for Manila.

"All aboard!" The blast of a whistle followed the conductor's familiar call. I gazed at the extraordinarily large setting sun as it shone orange light through the windows and warmed my face. I watched the farm fade into the horizon, then sat back in my seat and let the feeling of freedom wash over me.

Chapter 6

A New Beginning

I stepped off the train and onto the platform in Manila, looking around at the familiar station in the dim early-morning light. I recalled the many late nights I had spent there with Sonny and Joe, waiting to get the stale candies after the shopkeeper threw them out. I almost smiled at the thought. Around me, young kids were sleeping near the tracks, and teenagers were walking around aimlessly. Nothing had changed.

I was aching to see my brothers, but Pasay City was closer to the station, so I stopped by my old haunt first.

"Hey, where've you been?" Sonny said, jumping up to greet me as I approached. "I've been looking for you!"

"I've been working on a farm," I said, glad to see my old friend. "Where were you?! You were gone for a while."

"Oh, here and there," Sonny answered vaguely before quickly changing the subject.

"Listen," he said. "You gotta go back to the orphanage. People have been looking for you. Your brothers are going to America."

"What?"

"There are some American people who want to adopt you guys. You have to go so that they'll take you, too, or else they will leave you behind and you'll be stuck in this," he waved his arms around the slums, "forever!"

My jaw dropped, my mind reeling with the news. It was too much to take in. Adoption? America? It seemed too good to be true! I had heard stories about America, and whatever I knew about it was from the little television we saw at the orphanage.

In a daze and with many thoughts going through my head, I made my way slowly back to Kabataan, stopping to buy some candy along the way.

As the morning sun rose in the sky, I stood right in front of the gate, somehow unafraid of being snatched up by the house parents like I was before. Several kids recognized me and said, "Hey, they want you to go to America. These people are looking for you. They want to adopt you."

"Really?" I said. It still did not quite sink in. I was still focused on seeing my brothers so I could give them the candy.

"Butch! Butch!" Bobby and Adriano raced up to me, shouting with excitement and throwing their arms around me.

"Where were you?" they asked, grins stretched across their faces.

"I've been working on a farm," I said. "Here, I brought this for you." I gave them each a handful of candy. They beamed.

"You've been gone a long, long time," Adriano said through a mouthful of candy. "We were waiting for you forever!"

"How long has it been?" I wondered out loud, chewing on candy.

"A year, year and a half, something like that," Adriano mumbled as he opened another piece of candy. Happy to see his older brother at last, yet unsure and worried whether his brother would stick around, he said to me, "So you're coming back, right? You heard that some people from the United States want to adopt us? You're coming, right?"

"Sure," I said vaguely. I did not believe it would actually happen, and I sure as heck did not want to go back inside Kabataan. I did not quite trust the situation. I knew that kids sometimes got adopted, but it happened only now and then, and no one ever adopted three kids at once. In fact, the other kids used to taunt us about it, so I had put the thought of adoption out of my mind a long time ago. So was it really true that one family wanted to adopt all three of us? I could not be sure. What if it was a trick to get me back into the orphanage?

These thoughts swarmed through my mind as Adriano rambled about everything I had missed. I could not concentrate—I kept looking at Bobby, who seemed very sad and lonely. I worried about what might have happened to Bobby while I was gone. At least Adriano seemed fine.

After a few more minutes of chatting with my brothers, I told them I had to go do some stuff but would be back.

"OK, but you're coming back, right?" implored Adriano.

"See you again soon," I said.

My brothers were sad to see me go, and I was sad to leave, but I could not bring myself to go back into Kabataan just yet, no matter what everyone was saying.

Later that day, I ran into Sonny again while looking through the trash in the street, just as I had done before.

"You have to go back to the orphanage" were the first words out of Sonny's mouth. "I know what you're thinking—but it's a good place to be. People will adopt you and take you to America." He said this with both of his hands on my shoulders, looking me squarely in the eye.

I looked at Sonny, who I had always trusted through all these years. I looked at the cans I had just picked up from the trash and thought of all the millions of reasons why I had left Kabataan and vowed never to go back. I remembered clearly all the violence and abuse that occurred within that barbed-wire fence. Then I thought of my brothers going to America without me.

"OK," I said. "I will go back now."

If there is one thing I had learned at a young age, it was that whenever an opportunity presented itself, I had to take the ball and run with it. I had struggled with my emotions and fears over the previous week, ever since hearing the news about the possible adoption. I was scared of giving up my freedom and going back to the place I had left behind. All of these thoughts whirled through my head throughout the night and accompanied me on the long walk back to Kabataan. I did not know what would happen, but I knew I did not want to be left behind.

When I arrived at the orphanage later that day, I hesitated at the gate. What would they do to me? Would I be punished for leaving? I shuddered at the thought of another whipping or being forced to sit with me knees in salt. I almost ran away.

"I'm here," I said to Mrs. Santacruz, who was still behind the reception desk. "I'm back."

She looked up. "It's a good thing you are here," she said without greeting me, "because your brothers were not going without you."

"Are we really being adopted?" I asked her.

"Yes," she said. "There is a family in America that wants to adopt all of you. They would have taken just your brothers because it is easier to adopt two instead of three, but your brothers insisted that they would not leave without you…even though they had no idea where you were or if you'd even be back."

A pang of guilt shot through me at her last words, but overall I was just so happy that we were going to be adopted. I had always imagined America to be like Disney World (from what we saw on TV)—friendly and inviting, filled with warm people. There was no nervousness or apprehensiveness. I was just thrilled that I could finally be with my brothers and out of the Kabataan!

"You'll be in Cottage Five with Adriano and Bobby," she said. "You know the way." With that, she lowered her head and returned to her paperwork.

The next few months were a flurry of activity as doctors and social workers doted over us, inspecting us and asking all kinds of questions. It was strange and overwhelming. We were examined from head to toe. The doctors gave us medication to help the scabies, and we were given shot after stinging shot in our skinny arms. Our heads were shaved to get rid of lice before going to America.

I was mesmerized by the doctors, and I noticed how people seemed to listen to everything they said. As the doctor placed a wooden stick on my tongue, I was dazzled by the fancy gold watch that sparkled on the doctor's wrist. If I really got to America, I decided that I would study really hard and become a doctor when I grew up. That way, people would admire me and respect me. They would come to me for help. I would be needed and appreciated.

I also was not used to talking to social workers. It was weird to have adults suddenly paying attention to me. My brothers and I were withdrawn and quiet whenever the social workers asked questions, but we perked up when we were taken outside of the orphanage to go shopping for clothes. That was when I realized that we were really going to go to America. Afterward, the social worker took pictures of all three of us in our new clothes.

"This is so your new family can see what you look like," she told us.

We were happy. We had seen kids getting adopted now and then, but it was always just one kid at a time, and usually a pretty young kid. The kid would get his picture taken by a white person, and then he would be adopted and whisked away. That was always the procedure. Now that it was happening to us, we were ecstatic because we knew the adoption was for real. Luck was finally coming our way. I wondered if it was luck. I was not sure, but I did not care; we were going to America! From what we had seen on TV, America represented freedom, opportunity, and just about everything that the Kabataan did not offer us.

The other kids at the orphanage were happy but envious of us. The bullies finally left us alone. It was almost as if just by knowing we were to be adopted and going to America, we were protected. We finally felt safe!

Months later, the paperwork was finally finished. One morning, we were told to put on our new jeans instead of our cotton shorts. We packed our few possessions (mostly our new clothes) into clean bags, and then we were ushered onto a large bus with a social worker.

We grew more and more excited as the bus pulled up to a large building with giant, winged machines parked all around it.

"Is that a plane?" Bobby asked quietly, pointing to one of the machines that was slowly moving along a vast stretch of pavement.

"I don't know," I said. "I've never seen one before."

With our noses pressed up against the dirty glass windows, we marveled at all the strange things we saw and exclaimed about the size of everything.

After walking through the airport and spending a long time waiting on the hard seats, a voice came on the loudspeaker, and we were led onto the tarmac. Our excitement mounted as we climbed up a tall staircase, entering the huge machine that hummed underneath our feet. The social worker buckled us into our seats. We did not know what was going to happen next.

After a lot of people got on board the plane and sat down, the plane slowly started to move. My brothers and I strained to look out the windows at the buildings and cars moving past. The plane went faster and faster until everything outside became a blur, and then it lifted off the ground! I could not believe it. The plane rose higher and higher into the sky until the buildings became so small I could not see them anymore. I wondered what Sonny was doing and imagined that he was just a tiny speck below. Eventually the plane got so high that we could no longer see the ground anymore. With my mouth open, I stared at the white fluffy clouds floating past my window. It was the coolest thing I had ever seen.

With my hands trembling with excitement, I unbuckled my seatbelt and then my two brothers' seatbelts as well. We raced up and down the aisles of the plane, shouting with joy: "We are free! We're going to America!"

Someone grabbed me from behind and took my brothers and me back to our seats.

"Stay seated throughout the flight," the social worker told us in a firm voice, buckling me down.

I was excited and scared at the same time. I did not know what to expect, but I knew that anything outside of the orphanage would be better than being stuck there.

For the first time in my life, my future began to feel promising.

Part II
America

Chapter 7

The Mays

I fidgeted in my seat as the plane eased onto the runway at O'Hare International Airport in Chicago. Pressing my nose against the window, I gazed in awe at the cluster of tall buildings crammed along the river, jutting up toward the sky. As the plane coasted to a stop, my brothers and I smiled broadly at each other as the social worker unbuckled our seatbelts. *We were actually in America!*

Walking through the airport was a fascinating experience. I had never seen so many white people before. There were tall ones, skinny ones, short ones, and fat ones. They had hair of all colors—white, blond, orange, red, brown, black, and silver. Most of them wore nice clothes and carried expensive-looking suitcases. I wondered if they were all rich. They were all speaking English, which I did not understand at all. We stayed close to the social worker, who led the way and did all the talking.

After we got through Immigration and Passport Control, the social worker led us to the International Arrivals area where an excited couple stood up from their seats as we approached.

"Hello, boys!" said a plump lady with puffy, curly hair, opening her arms. "Did you have a good trip?" She gave each of us a hug. She smelled fresh and clean, like flowers. "Call me Mama," she whispered in my ear as she held me.

"Hello, sons," said the man standing next to her, smiling. He was a big, beefy guy with light brown hair on both sides of his head but no hair on top. He towered over us, and beaming down to us he said, "Ready to go to your new home?"

We did not understand a word because we did not speak any English. We stared at the strange white people and did not know how to reply, so we said nothing. We assumed that this couple must be our new parents because they were being so nice to us. My brothers and I looked at each other excitedly and spoke in our native Tagalog. Mr. and Mrs. Mays exchanged glances over our heads.

"This way, boys," Mr. Mays said, leading the new family to the parking garage.

We climbed into the station wagon, excited about being in a real car. It did not matter that the car was a bit old and the upholstery was a bit worn; we did not care. We had seen plenty of cars on the streets of Manila but had never ridden in one. The car was much smaller than a jeepney or a bus, but at least we did not have to share it with a bunch of other people, so we were happy.

As Mr. Mays pulled onto the highway toward Green Bay, we stared out the window and pointed at everything, captivated by the glittering lights of the city. Mr. Mays glanced at us in the rearview mirror and smiled as we talked away in Tagalog. When small flurries of snow started softly falling, our excitement mounted. Although Mrs. Mays could not understand what we were saying, she could tell by the sudden rise in volume that we had never seen snow before. She chuckled in amusement at our innocent delight.

Despite our elation, it was not long before we could no longer fight off the exhaustion of the long journey. We had not slept on the sixteen-hour plane ride because we had been too hyperactive from the adventure, but now the change in time zones was catching up with us. One by one, we dropped off to sleep, sprawled across the back seats of the station wagon as our new father drove us toward our new home.

"Kids, we're home," Anne Mays said, gently waking us. I sat up and rubbed my eyes. We stepped out from the warm car into the cold night. I shivered;

I had never been so cold before. The temperature was in the forties, but we did not have any jackets because no one had thought to buy any.

As Robert Mays unpacked the car, I noticed the white, soft-looking blanket of snow that covered the ground. "What is that?" I wondered, running toward it. I knelt down and touched it. The crystalline particles crumbled beneath my hands. Delighted, I ran across the yard as Adriano and Bobby joined me, leaving three sets of footprints as we shouted with joy. Laughing, we reached down and scooped up handfuls of snow, never noticing the icy sting on our bare hands, and threw the snow up into the air, jumping up and down as it landed on our heads and shoulders. As we frolicked in the snow, I noticed something strange: whenever I laughed or spoke, a white puff escaped from my mouth and vanished into the air. I had never seen anything like it.

"Come on, now," Anne called out to us, motioning for us to join her. "You'll catch a cold out there!"

As the five of us walked toward the front door, I noticed the house for the first time. I stopped in the driveway and stared in awe at our new home. It was far bigger than I could have imagined, although I would later realize that it was just an average-sized American home. I was impressed by its solid brick construction and nice windows.

I gazed down the street of Kaukauna, Wisconsin. The other houses we passed were just the same. Every house had a car in front, and a couple of them had two cars. None of the houses had brick walls topped with broken glass, though, and as far as I could see, there weren't any piles of trash anywhere. *It must not be trash night*, I thought.

"Butch!" Robert called out to me from the front door. "Come on, let's get inside!"

The voice of my new father shook me out of my reverie. Quickly I raced up the driveway and into the house.

"And here's your room," Robert said, flicking on the switch. I peered inside. The basement room was small but cozy. I walked in and touched the wooden desk and sat on the edge of the small bed, looking around. On one side of the room was a bookshelf, and on the other side was a bureau with three drawers.

"Do you like it?" Robert beamed at me from the doorway.

"Make yourself at home," Anne said. "You know where the bathroom is, so you can help yourself when you need to. We'll see you in the morning."

She winked at me and softly closed the door. As soon as they were gone, I stood up and inspected everything in the room. I opened all the drawers and looked under the bed, and then I flipped through some of the books left on the bookshelf. I wondered what my brothers were doing in their rooms. We had never had our own bedrooms before; Adriano and Bobby were used to sleeping with each other, and I had gotten used to sleeping on the street or the hut. It felt strange to have an actual bed to sleep in—all by myself. I half-expected Bobby to crawl into bed with me that night, as he'd done so many times at the orphanages.

As I lay in bed in the dark, I was too excited to sleep, even though I was exhausted after the day traveling. My thoughts were racing a mile a minute. The mattress was so soft underneath me, it felt like I was lying on a cloud. The room was quiet, even quieter than sleeping in the bamboo hut at the farm, because I could not hear any frogs or crickets. I tried to sleep, but I kept thinking about what I had left behind in the Philippines. I thought of Sonny and Joe and wondered if they had found anything good in the trash. I thought of my parents and wondered if I would ever see them again.

I felt sharp pricks behind my eyes at the thought of my parents. I tried to hold them back, but the tears persisted. On my first night in America, I cried myself to sleep, as I had done so many nights in my home country.

One of the first things the Mays did was take us out shopping for new clothes. We had brought almost no clothes with us, so we each got a whole new wardrobe: shirts, pants, shorts, socks, and underwear (this was the first time we wore underwear!). We got a few pairs of each, as well as new sweaters and jackets. It was more clothes than I had ever owned in my entire life. I was proud to wear my clean new clothes. I thought back to the stained, torn clothes I wore when I lived on the streets in Pasay City, and I cringed. In the Mays' house, every time something I wore got dirty, I simply threw it into a basket, and a few days later it appeared in my bureau, freshly cleaned and neatly folded. It was miraculous.

Our first week in the United States was a whirlwind of new experiences. Life in America was so different from what we were used to back in the Philippines, so everything was a novelty.

Meals were one of our biggest sources of pleasure and discovery. To start with, we were simply thrilled about having so much food to eat. To go to bed without hunger pangs was pure luxury. At the dinner table, Robert and Anne marveled at our appetites. "I don't understand how these boys are so skinny—they eat so much!" Anne remarked to Robert as they watched us wolf down hamburgers and French fries and noisily slurp on milkshakes. The first time we went through the drive-thru at A&W Burgers, we were flabbergasted to hear the strange sounds coming from the square box that Robert spoke into. When the box responded, it actually seemed like Robert and the box were having a conversation! Minutes later, he pulled the car up to a window, and someone handed him a few bags that smelled divine. We did not know what was in the bags, but our mouths started watering from the smell of it.

The Mays drove home and distributed the food, handing us paper plates to eat on. The hamburgers were so tasty, each bite seemed to tantalize taste buds I didn't even know I had. It was so different than the bland soup we had been fed at Kabataan.

When we finished eating, we went to the sink and started washing the paper plates, as we had seen Anne do with the plastic plates that she kept stacked in the cupboard. This time Anne laughed. "No, boys," she said, walking over, because she knew we would not understand what she was saying. "You don't wash paper plates; you throw them away!" She demonstrated by pitching her used paper plate into the small trash can in the corner. We watched her in disbelief. In the Philippines, we washed and reused paper plates over and over until they fell apart. Right away, we could see that life in the United States was going to be different.

During our first weeks in Wisconsin, we sampled every typically American dish that the Mays could think of: pizza, hot dogs, spaghetti with meatballs, corn on the cob, mashed potatoes with gravy, green bean casserole, fast-food burritos, macaroni and cheese, meatloaf, apple pie, peanut butter and jelly sandwiches, and of course, hamburgers and french fries with ketchup. Every meal was a feast compared to what we were fed at Kabataan and what I had eaten on the streets.

At first, we ate everything with our hands because that was what we were used to doing. When the Mays burst into laughter as we tried to eat spaghetti with our hands, we realized that Americans eat most of their food with a fork or a spoon. By copying the Mays' actions, my brothers and I learned which foods were meant to be eaten with a fork or spoon and which foods were OK to pick up with our fingers.

Not long after arriving at the Mays' house (sometime in April), Robert led us to the driveway. He ducked into the open garage and wheeled out two small Huffy bikes as Anne brought out a third one. My eyes widened. *Could this really be? My own bike?!* I beamed, remembering how much I had enjoyed riding the rental bike back in Manila. I hopped on the bike and pedaled up and down the street, enjoying this two-wheeled freedom. The bikes were new and looked fancy. They were a lot better than the one I had rented in Manila. I watched as Robert, Anne, and the Mays' son-in-law, Randy, patiently taught my brothers how to ride.

After Adriano and Bobby figured out how to ride their bikes, we spent days riding around the neighborhood together, exploring our new surroundings. The neighborhood vaguely reminded me of the neighborhood where our aunt lived because the houses were nice. These houses were bigger than Filipino houses, though, and no one seemed to keep pigs or chickens in their backyards.

On my bike travels, I was struck by how clean Wisconsin was compared to where I had come from. Aside from a few empty soda cans or fast-food wrappers here and there, the roads were always cleared of trash. At first I could not wrap my head around the concept of throwing trash into a big plastic bag, then tying up that bag and throwing it into a large metal can with a circular lid, then dragging that large, heavy can to the end of the sidewalk once a week. It seemed like an odd ritual because if the garbage was all tied away inside bags, how would the street kids pick through it? The thought plagued me for weeks until I began to realize that maybe there weren't any street kids in Kaukauna, Wisconsin. To ease my mind, I set out to look for them. But no matter how far I rode my bike, I never saw any street kids with matted hair and dirty, torn clothes. I decided that Wisconsin must be a pretty nice place if the kids did not need to pick through trash to make money or to eat.

The language barrier was the first hurdle faced by the five us in our new family. Anne and Robert were eager to get to know us, but it was difficult because communication did not flow smoothly.

I learned later that when the Mays first initiated the process of bringing us over to the United States through Holt International Children's Services, they had been counseled in-depth about the potential difficulties they might face as a new family. They were warned about the challenges that could arise from not speaking the same language. Cultural differences between the States and the Philippines could also pose obstacles to understanding one another. Lastly, the social worker made it clear that children like us might have problems adjusting to our new environment, especially being part of a family after so many years of neglect. "The emotional scars from their abandonment might run deeper then you'd think," the Mays had been advised.

Robert and Anne nodded and said they understood, assuming that these issues could be easily overcome with a bit of love and kindness…but the reality is not always as we envision it.

Anne Mays stood at the kitchen sink, watching us eat down hot dogs and potato chips as we chatted away in Tagalog, laughing uproariously between bites.

She smiled sadly, but we barely noticed. We had been in her house for a couple of weeks but were like strangers because we could not communicate much beyond the bare basics.

"I can't take it anymore," she said to Robert in a hushed tone. "I cannot understand them, and they cannot understand me."

He put his hands on her shoulders "It's OK," he said, kissing her cheek. "It takes time. Here is what we'll do: we will ban Tagalog from the house. That will help them learn English quicker, and it will be better for them in the long run."

Robert and Anne sat down with us at kitchen table, watching as we licked the salt off our fingertips, the crumpled potato-chip bag completely empty. Robert cleared his throat. We stopped talking and looked at him.

"English," Robert said. "Speak English only from now on. You are not allowed to speak Tagalog in this house anymore. No Tagalog. Understand?" He looked at us closely. We looked at him then looked at each other. We shrugged and nodded but had no idea what he had said.

From then on, any time one of us was "caught" speaking our native tongue, Anne or Robert would say "No" and shake their heads firmly. "English," they would say. Eventually, Tagalog was stamped from our minds completely.

Watching TV became one of our primary methods for picking up the English language. It was practically an evening ritual at the Mays household. After dinner, Robert and Anne enjoyed cracking open a can of beer

My Third Parents

and watching their favorite programs. We liked watching shows such as the Tom and Jerry Show.

Although we did not understand anything at first, it was still fun to watch TV because it was a brand-new experience. We seldom got to watch TV in the Philippines because the orphanage had only one TV that we had to share with more than 150 children. The television also became an important way for us to learn about American culture. From studying the people on the various shows and commercials, we learned about the latest American fashions, as well as the typical social etiquette.

By listening to the sounds spoken on the television, we began to understand the rhythm of the language, and soon we were able to pick out individual words and entire phrases. Our new parents helped us learn English by speaking slowly. At the dinner table, they pointed to specific things, such as cups, plates, and hot dogs, and said the word for each thing in English. Then we would repeat them. At times it was challenging, but it was also kind of fun.

After I met Anne's sister and her kids, I enjoyed learning English from them, too.

One day, a van pulled up to the Mays' residence, and three kids piled out. "Uncle Robert! Aunt Anne! We're here!" they shouted as they spilled out of the van into the yard. The youngest was around my age, and the other two were a couple of years older. A man and woman stepped out of the van and walked up to us. "You must be my sister's new kids!" the woman exclaimed, getting a good look at us.

"This is Fernando, the oldest," Anne said to her sister. "And this is Adriano, the middle brother. And here is Bobby, the youngest."

"Bobby—he's my boy!" Robert Mays said, tickling him. "Robert Junior, he is!" Bobby giggled. He did not understand what was being said, but he could sense the lightheartedness of the occasion, and it made him happy.

"Boys, this is your Aunt Linda and Uncle Ben. Linda is my sister," Anne explained slowly. "And these are their kids: Matt, Karin, and Dawn."

"Hey, wanna play a game?" Matt asked us.

"They don't speak much English, so you'll have to teach them," Anne said.

"That's OK," Don said. "We'll teach 'em to play tag or something—that's easy!"

———

Anne and Linda watched us chasing each other around the front yard as they sipped their coffee at the kitchen table.

"So, explain to me the whole process again. You brought all three of them over from the Philippines?" Linda asked her sister. "You and Robert paid for them to come here?"

"That's right. We want to adopt them. Right now they are our foster kids. We are temporary guardians. There's a whole other process for adopting them, so we'll go through that soon."

"How are you arranging all this? It sounds like a lot of paperwork. How do you know what to do?"

"We're working with an adoption agency. I'll show you the brochure later. They organized everything for us, and they're walking us through all the steps—all the legal mumbo jumbo and everything."

Anne smiled as she watched me topple over Matt on the lawn, laughing.

"We love having them here. You know how much I love kids. With our daughters all grown up and out of the house, it was starting to feel so empty. It's nice having the boys around."

"I'm glad it's all working out so far. Is everything turning out like you wanted it to?"

"So far things are great," Anne said. "The boys seem so excited to be here. They love TV, and you should have seen their faces the first time we went through a McDonald's drive-thru!"

Anne and her sister laughed.

"Well, I am more than happy to welcome them to our family," Linda said. "There's enough room in our van, so we'll take 'em up to visit Mom in Peshtigo next weekend. And they'll love going out to the cabin in Iron Mountain."

"Did someone say Iron Mountain?" Ben said as he and Robert walked into the kitchen.

"Yep, I was just telling Anne that we'll take her boys on road trips with us. That way our kids will have some company, too."

"Oh, yeah!" said Ben, sipping on his beer. "They'll have fun berry picking in the summers, and in the winters they will love snowmobiling! I bet they never did that in the Philippines!"

The fondest memories I had with the Mays were with my cousins, Matt, Karin, and Dawn. They were our playmates. They thought us about being a child in America. We spent a lot of fun times camping in northern Wisconsin, enjoying barbecue and great fireworks on the fourth of July.

Uncle Ben was funny and had an easygoing personality as did Aunt Linda; they were very kind to us.

When my brothers and I showed up at the Green Bay Area Public School District, no one knew what to do with us. They were not used to processing foreign students. After much deliberation, I was placed into the fifth grade at MacArthur Elementary School, even though I was three years older than the other kids in the class.

Going to school with all the other kids was a strange experience—it was like a novice swimmer being thrown into the deep end of a pool. The lessons were overwhelming, and I was completely lost because I did not understand 95 percent of what was being said. On top of my difficulties with my classes, I also learned that the kids at school were not as welcoming as my new cousins.

"Gook!" called a voice as I was riding my bike home from MacArthur Elementary School.

"Chink!"

I turned my head. Some of the fifth-graders from my class were riding their bikes home at a slow pace behind me. They snickered when I turned around. One of them made a rude sign with his fingers. "Go back to where you belong!" the little boy sneered.

I felt my face growing red and shouted at them in Tagalog, which made them laugh harder. At thirteen, I was extremely cognizant of what I looked like compared to the other kids at the predominantly white school. I was acutely aware that my skin was darker than that of most of the people in Green Bay, including my new family. I felt like I stuck out, and some kids wasted no time in letting me know that I was different.

I stopped my bike and swerved around, then pedaled toward them at full speed. I did not understand what they were saying, but I knew that their words were not nice. As I approached, the other boys laughed and veered off down a side street, shouting names as they fled through neighbors' yards.

I did not bother following them. I did not know the neighborhood as well as they did, and I was smart enough to realize that they could trick me by leading me into some kind of trap. I was outnumbered anyway.

When I got home that day, I handed Anne the note that the school nurse had given me. Adriano and Bobby had received the same notes from the nurse, too.

"Head lice," Anne said, sighing after reading the notes, which she handed to her husband. "They've been suspended for ten days."

Robert grunted, then crumpled the notes and tossed them into the trash can as they both left the room. We stood looking at each other, bewildered. We had no idea what was going on.

I awoke the next day, Tuesday, at 10:00 am. When my eyes fell on the clock next to my bed, I sprang up, threw on some clothes, and raced upstairs. *Why didn't they wake me up for school?* I wondered. When I reached the kitchen, Adriano was already sitting at the kitchen table finishing his cereal as Anne nonchalantly sipped her morning coffee.

"School?" I asked Anne, pointing to the clock. "Late?"

"No school," Anne said. "No school today."

As I crunched on my breakfast, I wondered if we were being punished for something. *Maybe it has something to do with those notes*, I thought, remembering their strange reaction the day before. *Are we in trouble?*

After breakfast, Anne showed us a long, plastic bottle. "Shampoo," she said slowly. "You put it on your hair, rub it around, and rinse it off." She mimed squeezing whatever was in the bottle onto the palm of her hand and rubbing it all over her head. Then she sent us into the shower one by one, with the hope that we would understand and follow her instructions. I thought it was a bit strange; I had never used shampoo in my life. Until then, I did not even know what it was.

After a few days of staying at home, I started to get worried that we were not allowed to go to school at all anymore. I did not have the words to ask Anne, but I would not have understood the explanation anyway with my limited English. Those two weeks at home were hard for me because I sensed that my new mother was ashamed of us for some reason. My brothers and I felt ostracized and uncomfortable in the house, as if we had done something wrong. Only much later did I realize that lice were considered dirty and unhygienic. Then I understood why all the kids in the orphanages always had their heads shaved.

It was my first uncomfortable experience in the Mays household. By that time, the newness of everything was starting to fade for everyone.

Although I had trouble fitting in at school, eventually I made friends with a boy named Jamie, who lived down the street. As I rode my bike past a large green field, Jamie called me over.

"Hey, we need another teammate! Wanna play soccer?"

I jumped off my bike, happy to be included in something. I did not know what they were playing, but I understood that there were two goals, one on each end of the field. I enjoyed racing up and down the field with the other kids, chasing after the ball. As it soared through the air, I positioned myself underneath it, catching it before it hit the ground. Then I took off running toward the goal.

"Hey! You can't do that!" someone shouted.

I stopped and turned around.

"That's against the rules!" the kid yelled again, pointing at the soccer ball in my hands.

I threw down the ball and tore after the kid, punching him in the stomach before the kid even knew what hit him. I had no idea what the kid had said, but I was sensitive about being yelled at in that tone because so many kids at school yelled at me and teased me, calling me names all the time. I had assumed this kid was just another jerk.

"Fernando, stop it!" Jamie said, racing between me and the other kid. "Leave him alone. Calm down."

The other kid glared at me as Jamie slowly explained the rules. "In soccer, you cannot touch the ball with your hands," he tried to make it as clear as possible in language I could understand. "No hands. OK?"

"OK," I said, nodding. "No hands."

I got into those kinds of misunderstandings all too easily because I still could not understand what other kids were saying to me, even if they were just being harmless. Anytime someone yelled at me, I thought they were picking on me. I had my honor to uphold—I did not want anyone to get away with calling me names. I knew how bullies operated and how dangerous it could be to look weak. I had already suffered too much in life to put up with that kind of abuse.

I spent my first summer in the United States roaming the neighborhood streets on my Huffy bike. By the time school let out, I had made a few more friends around the neighborhood, so we rode around together and played games in the summer heat.

That was also the summer that the movie *ET* came out. The blockbuster film sparked my imagination as I watched the adventure unfold on the giant screen. After that, I loved to ride my bike through the streets and pretend that I was soaring through the sky with a small alien friend in my front basket.

As the long, hot summer lazily yawned to a close, a notice arrived in the mail from the school board. After a year at MacArthur Elementary School, I was being forced to go straight to high school, even though I was not ready. My English was still paltry, and I was academically far behind the other kids who would be in my freshman class. But as far as the school district was concerned, because I was about to turn fifteen, I was too old to be in fifth grade again. So the Mays enrolled me in the ninth grade at Southwest High School for the fall of 1982. I looked forward to being with kids my own age—especially girls—but the idea also was daunting to me.

High school was a whole new territory. The kids were bigger, the school was huge, and there was a whole new set of social protocol that I was entirely unfamiliar with. Thanks to puberty, I was painfully aware of my appearance and self-conscious about how others, especially girls, would see me. I did not know what kind of clothes to wear, and I struggled to fit in. I made a few friends, but I did not really know how the whole social scene worked. It was confusing. I'd spent so many years of my life focused on survival, concentrating on just getting through the day with enough food, that I didn't know how to relate when I was suddenly thrown in with kids my age whose biggest concerns were what to wear or how to get rid of their pimples.

At least my teachers were helpful and understanding. They had all been briefed that I had recently come over from the Philippines and that my English was not very good, so they knew not to be too hard on me during class if I lagged behind the other students. I was determined to master English, so twice a week in the evenings I took the bus from Southwest High School, which I attended regular classes, to West High School, which was the only place that offered ESL (English as a Second Language) courses. Between regular classes and ESL classes, I stayed very busy throughout the week. Sometimes at lunch I sat with the geeks and smart kids, flipping through my ESL books as they did their algebra and trig homework.

For the most part, the kids at school were friendly, but occasionally I ran into some problems with ignorant, racist bullies.

"Out of my way, you gook," someone growled in a gruff voice, pushing me from behind.

I whipped around defiantly and looked the kid in the eyes. The kid was bigger than me, but most kids were, anyway, so I did not care. Without a second thought, I hit the kid square in the nose. Blood spurted everywhere. As the bully held his face, I said, "OK, after school, let's go outside. We'll fight." I gave the kid the meanest look I could muster. *I'll show him not to mess with me*, I thought.

After school, I waited…and waited. I was scared and took a wooden stick with me. The bully never showed up, so I walked home feeling like a champion. That bully never bothered me again!

That was not the only bully I encountered, though. In homeroom, I sat next to a kid named Brian who teased me mercilessly every day, usually muttering obscenities under his breath loud enough for me to hear but quiet enough that the teacher did not notice. Brian teased me about everything, from my face to my hair to my clothes to the way I spoke English. With the teacher in the room, I tried to ignore him, but one day Brian taunted me before the bell rang. I seized my chance, pummeling Brian with my fists until he was bleeding, but Brian defiantly continued to call me names.

My Third Parents

"Stop it, you guys!" shouted a couple of the girls in the room as they clutched their notebooks to their chests. I could not tell which bothered them more: the blood dripping from Brian's cut lip or the fact that Brian was spouting nasty remarks at one of their classmates.

"Cut it out, Brian," snapped a handsome, dark-haired boy named Mark. "You're an idiot, you know that?"

Brian looked at Mark, who was much more popular than he was, and finally shut his mouth.

Mark turned to me. "Ignore that moron," he said.

I nodded at him and managed a smile. "Thanks, Mark.

After that, Mark and I became friends. Mark liked that I was different from the other kids. He did not see my differences as a bad thing at all. In fact, he found it interesting. Mark asked questions about where I was from and whether the Philippines were a lot different from Wisconsin. I answered his questions, happy to make a new friend, but carefully left out all the parts about living on the streets and picking through garbage.

"What kind of clothes did you wear in the Philippines?" Mark asked tactfully.

"Usually shorts and a T-shirt," I said. "It was always pretty hot there."

"Ah," said Mark, assessing my outfit. "Why don't you come over to my house today after school? We are about the same size. You can borrow some of my stuff."

I was excited and pleased at this new friendship. Mark was popular for a reason: not only was he handsome and friendly, but he had style. I was eager to expand my wardrobe and grateful for my friend's generosity. At Mark's house, I tried on baggy silk shirts, leather ties, and parachute pants. Mark's clothes were much more expensive than the clothes the Mays could afford.

"Looking good!" Mark said, plunking a pair of dark sunglasses onto my face and turning me toward the mirror. I smiled.

Not long into the school year, my eyes fell upon the most beautiful girl I had ever seen. She had the blond hair of an angel (just like my cousin, Dawn), with tightly permed curls held in place by hairspray. Her eyes rivaled the blue of the deepest ocean. I first noticed her on the bus that went from the west side of Green Bay to the east side—my twice-weekly bus trip for my ESL classes. I could barely speak any English, so I did not know how to profess my love, but one day our eyes met as we both stood up to exit the bus. When she smiled at me, I knew I was in love.

Julia was my first girlfriend, although technically she was not allowed to date, so it was not official. She was only fourteen, and I was fifteen. We began to meet secretly at the bus stop on her side of town, and then I walked her home, but I was never allowed in, so our secret rendezvous were all too short. I enjoyed practicing my English with her, struggling to find the words to express the affection in my heart, while she laughed and corrected me. Every time she looked at me with her twinkling blue eyes, I melted.

Before we reached her block, I put my arms around her gently and gave her a kiss on her soft lips, relishing the warm sensation that spread through my body. She was the first girl I had ever kissed. The feeling of her lips and the softness of her body stayed with me long after we departed.

She called me almost every day, and we talked, even though it was a lopsided conversation because I did not have full command of the English language yet.

I relished the feeling of liking someone and being liked back. I had never realized how good it could feel because I'd never been shown affection before. However, after several weeks of puppy love, I was going broke. I did not have enough money to take the bus to the other side of town for all of those extra trips; I had only enough change to go over for my ESL lessons. Besides, our forbidden romance was going nowhere. So one day I didn't called her back. It broke my heart to know that she would be devastated, but it was simply easier to not return her call than it was to try to explain all of this to her in my broken English.

My Third Parents

The next time I stepped off the bus on the west side of town attend my ESL class, she was not there waiting for me as she usually was. The romance was over.

Bobby watched me writhing on the floor, spinning in circles and kicking my legs into the air.

"What are you doing?" he asked, mystified.

"It's called break dancing," I said, getting back into my moves. I tried to study my movements in the mirror, comparing it with the Michael Jackson videos I had seen on TV.

Bolstered by my first girlfriend and first kiss, I was eager for another one. I might not be the smartest, smoothest, or most stylish boy in school, but at least I could be the hottest guy on the dance floor. I had rhythm.

School dances provided me with the opportunity to shine. Every time I got down on the floor and started flailing about in time to the music, the other kids formed a circle around me, cheering me on and clapping. I loved the attention. It made me feel accepted, like I belonged. Yet, despite the whoops and cheers I received on the dance floor, I was not having any luck finding another girlfriend.

High school often felt like a long struggle to fit in. The other kids had the advantage of being brought up in America, so they knew the ropes. They knew what to say and do, how to act, and how to dress. I did not understand how these things worked, especially the dating scene. I wanted to ask girls out, but I did not know how. In my ESL lessons, I sat tapping my pencil against my lip, wondering if I could gather up the courage after class to ask the ESL teacher what phrases would be handy for asking someone out on a date. I never did. So after my brief romance with the girl from the bus stop, I did not date for another two years. That does not mean I did not try, though. I was never one to give up.

During winter break, I hung out with a few friends at Mark's house. There were four of us, three boys and one girl, a beautiful brunette named Sandy. Mark's parents were not home, so through a connection with an older brother, we managed to get a case of Pabst Beer.

That night was my first time getting drunk since my experience with gin when I was eleven. This time, it was much more fun, though. I did not throw up. Instead I talked and laughed with my friends late into the night, admiring the melody of Sandy's laughter and the way her eyes crinkled when she smiled.

Sandy stood up and yawned. "All right, fellas," she said. "It's time to get home." She turned to me. "You need a ride? You live a couple streets over from my house, right?"

I did not need to be asked twice. I jumped at the chance.

"There are still a few cans of beer left," Mark said. "Who wants it?"

The other boy shook his head. "I can't take it. I'll get in trouble!"

That left me and Sandy. I wanted to impress her, so I said, "I'll take it. No problem." The guys grinned with relief.

I was nervous and excited on the car ride home, elated to be alone in the car with this beautiful creature. I wanted to pounce on her right away, but I used every ounce of will power to restrain myself. We talked and laughed on the way home, but I could not remember any of the conversation later. I was too drunk and giddy.

"OK, here you go!" she said with a giggle, stopping her car in front of the Mays' mailbox.

"Thank you for the ride home," I said.

"Oh, you're welcome," she said with a casual smile. "It was no problem."

With that, I seized the moment and leaned over to kiss her. She pulled away.

"Oh, we're just friends," she said quickly, blushing.

"Oh," I said. Her words hit like a blow. "OK. I am sorry."

"Good night," she said as I stepped out of the car with the beer in my hand.

I steadied myself on the sidewalk and walked up the driveway to my house, turning to wave good-bye as she drove away. Before going into the house, I hid the beer behind a bush so that I would not get in trouble. Quietly slipping the key into the lock, I entered the back door and let it close softly behind me.

The next morning, I stumbled up the stairs for breakfast. A six-pack of Pabst greeted me on the table, covered with a little bit of dirt. Anne and Robert sat in their chairs, sipping their morning coffee. They watched me with odd expressions, as if they were trying to repress their smiles, but could not.

"So, when were you gonna invite us to share this beer?" Anne said, trying to be stern, but smiling.

"Um...." I was for once at a loss for words. "It's not mine?"

"We saw you take it out of the car last night," Anne said with a smile. "You're grounded."

Grounded! I slumped into my chair at the table, groggily wondering why Anne and Robert were acting so amused about the whole thing. Why weren't they hitting the roof with anger? They made an effort to act disapproving, but their looks of contained excitement betrayed their true emotions. They were happy and relieved that I was making headway in the United States by socializing and making friends. Getting caught with beer was like a rite of passage; I was finally fitting in.

The next day, I discovered the empty Pabst beer cans in the trash. It looked like Anne and Robert enjoyed finishing off the confiscated goods.

I lugged a heavy book into the kitchen after dinner and set it on the table with a thud. "Mom, can you help me with my homework?"

"What's it about?" she asked.

"I have to figure out the sine and cosine, and there's something about pies," I said, flipping open the book.

She peered at the page. "Oh, it's math," she said. "Ask your dad for help."

"He said to ask you," I said.

"Oh," she said. "Well, use a calculator." With that, she went back to washing the dishes, humming to herself. The discussion was closed.

Every day, I brought home heavy textbooks. I spent evenings after dinner swamped with homework, struggling to understand the principles of economics and the impact of the Magna Carta, but it was difficult, especially because I struggled to understand even the basic verb conjugations in my textbooks. So much of what I was being taught at school was far beyond my comprehension, simply due to my limited English.

I craved someone who could guide me and tutor me in these subjects. I knew I could understand the rest of my subjects if I just had a better grasp of English. The Mays did not finish high school, let alone go to college, so they were not much help with school work. Anne had gotten pregnant with her oldest daughter, Barbara, while she was still in high school, so she had to drop out. When Barbara came to the house with her boyfriend, Randy, I sometimes asked them for help, but they did not know much, either.

"You know, that stuff is really not that important," Randy said, looking over the page of equations in my textbook. "You'll never use that stuff in real life—trust me." He punched me lightly on the forearm. "Hey, I will show you something useful. Come help me work on my truck."

Randy was a cool guy and a good role model to have around. He took me under his wing, as if I were his own little brother. He showed me how to work on cars and trucks, explaining all the parts under the hood and why they were important. It was not long before I started fantasizing about cars, flipping through car magazines and drawing different makes and models on plain white paper with a pencil. I carefully measured the proportions and tried to get the shading just right.

Anne noticed my drawing skills and handed me an ad she had found in the paper for art lessons. I applied to be a student. My drawing skills earned me a scholarship that paid for 50 percent of the tuition. I enjoyed the art classes because they helped me improve my natural abilities. I was proud of all the artwork I created for my art class, but most of all I admired a detailed drawing I made of a Los Angeles pitcher I had spent hours working on, perfecting the composition and shading.

At school I also took music lessons, learning to play the clarinet. I enjoyed my art and music classes more than the academic subjects because I did not need to have a strong command of English to learn which notes to play or figure out how to paint with watercolors. When I drew, I could express myself however I wanted. I was good at it, too. My teachers and the other kids at school noticed my art skills and complimented me on my drawings. Art and music became a form of nonverbal communication that gave me a sense of freedom and achievement while I struggled to learn English.

Although I enjoyed certain classes and was starting to make friends, I often felt like I was sinking deep into a black hole from which I could not escape. The despair that engulfed me in the Philippines still kept a tight clutch around my soul, no matter how hard I tried to be happy.

The joy of being in America, along with the ease and convenience that comes with the American lifestyle, was simply not enough to completely wash away the painful memories of years of abandonment, hunger, and abuse. I lay on my new bed and stared at the clean socks on my feet, remembering the many nights I had slept quietly on the floor of my bamboo hut. The memories and feelings flooded back and cascaded forth in tears.

Where are my real parents? I wondered. *Do they ever think about me? I'll never see them again, now that I'm in America. But why should I even care? They left me, after all. I am better off here with these people who are taking care of me. People who actually want me.*

I wiped away the tears and tried to brush the thoughts from my mind, but as hard as I tried, I could not dig myself out of these sad feelings that overwhelmed me. Adriano, Bobby, and I never spoke about the pain our parents caused us in the Philippines, but I often caught them with a sad expression similar to mine.

"Why did Mom leave us?" I wept, roaming the empty house while my parents and brothers were at a middle-school function. I missed my real mom—the mother who had abandoned me without looking back. *Why did she do this to us?* I could not explain why I missed my real mom so much—the woman who left me and my brothers and never returned. Even though I had not seen her in nine years, nearly a decade, the mere thought of her brought me to tears. I tried to be tough and stifle the pain, but I could not choke back the memories that flooded me when I was home alone. With the TV off and the radio silent, I could feel the dead air creeping in on me, closing in on all sides.

I had never been alone in an actual house before moving in with the Mays, only in my hut on the farm. When everyone was gone, I paced around the living room, trying to shake off my sadness. I walked along the row of family photographs lining the mantel—black and white photos of Anne's parents as children, sepia-toned images of Robert's grandparents, Anne and Robert on their wedding day, Anne laughing as Robert helped their young daughters build a snowman…. They were all photos I could not relate to. As far as I was concerned, it was as if I had no past. I knew nothing of my ancestors; I could barely remember my parents' faces.

I paused in front of the first family photo taken of me with the Mays and studied my smiling thirteen-year-old face that had beamed at the camera so brightly. My brothers and I wore matching plaid button-up shirts that we had been so proud to own after our first shopping spree in America. Our hair was neatly combed and tidy—we must have grasped the concept of shampoo by then. We all looked so clean-cut and happy, posing for the camera. However, I felt like it was a sham.

I felt like we did not genuinely belong on that wall of smiling, happy faces because we were too broken inside, too damaged from the past to be able to run from it and pretend it never happened. Our three smiling faces were unreal because they did not reveal the truth, the pain behind our eyes.

Even though I was nearly eight thousand miles away from Manila, I could not run away from the pain that crippled me during the night. I muffled my cries into my pillow, just as I had done at Kabataan. Even though

I was now in America, the pain of abandonment was very much alive and no easier to bear.

I could not stand to look at the photos any longer. I had to end it all. I crept into my parents' bedroom, tiptoeing respectfully even though they were not there. I went straight to the medicine cabinet in their bathroom, careful not to touch anything else. In a fit of tears, I opened every bottle I could find and popped all of the pills into my mouth. I swallowed so many pills I lost count. I did not even know what the labels said, but I hoped the cocktail of drugs would kill me.

I lay on my bed and waited for death to take me. With tears running down my cheeks, I thought about my brothers and sobbed harder. Who would take care of them when I was gone? It was my job to look after them—my dad said so. That was the last thing my dad ever said to me.

If it were not for those thoughts about my brothers, I would have tried harder to kill myself, but I think my love for them kept me alive.

Anne sat on her bed and wiped the frustrated tears from her eyes as Robert entered the room.

"What's wrong, hon?" he asked, sitting down next to her.

"Oh, I don't know," she sniffled. "It's just…it's so hard sometimes, trying to relate to those boys. I can't get through to them, and they don't seem to understand me. It's not a language thing anymore. I don't know what it is."

"They are difficult kids," Robert agreed.

"Plus, look what I found in the bathroom," Anne continued, angrily pointing at the half-dozen empty medicine bottles that she had thrown in the wastebasket. "I think it was Fernando. I don't know if he swallowed all of them or what. Maybe he is trying to sell the pills to kids at school or something. Either way, I feel like I failed as a parent," she cried hopelessly as Robert held her close.

"What are we doing wrong?" Robert murmured.

"I don't know…. We never had these problems when we raised our girls. God, I didn't know it would be like this."

"Maybe we're not the problem," Robert mused, "Maybe they are. We gave them a home to live in, clothes to wear, food to eat. Much more than they had in the Philippines. It's not our fault if they're having problems."

Moving to the United States and living with a new family was not an easy transition for me and my brothers, but it was not an easy adjustment for Anne and Robert, either. They had the best of intentions in taking us in, brimming with high hopes of welcoming us into their family with open arms. But the reality was simply overwhelming. In their enthusiasm, they did not fully comprehend that the three kids they wanted to adopt had already lived very intense lives in the Philippines—a culture that the Mays had no familiarity with at all.

Although Robert and Anne tried to be nurturing and understanding parents, there was no way they could relate to the traumatic experiences we had been through. In their minds, the orphanages might have been unpleasant—even terrible—places, but they could not fathom the extremity of our ordeal. They had no idea what it felt like for us to have been abandoned and neglected for so many years and to have languished in a violent orphanage where there was never enough food to eat.

Our lives in the Philippines were too far beyond their comprehension, so they never talked about it. They never considered that it might help us to get counseling. In a way, they simply preferred to pretend that our pasts never happened. It was easier for Robert and Anne to expect us to simply fit in; they did not know what to do. However, fitting in to a whole new culture and a whole new environment, let alone a whole new family and a whole new language, did not come easily at all for the three of us. The learning curve was too steep to expect an easy adjustment.

I was wearing two sweaters, but I was still freezing. The Mays could not afford to turn up the thermostat that winter. Robert was a subcontractor in the construction business, and no jobs were coming in. He was basically unemployed for a long stretch, although it was through no fault of his own. He had always worked hard to support his family, but at that moment, the job market looked bleak. Over previous winters, when Robert had an ample workload, I used to tag along and earn some extra money doing menial labor around the job site—but not this year. Anne was a stay-at-home mom, so she was not bringing in any income.

The family had to rely on government subsidies to make ends meet. They got an abundance of government cheese, so throughout the cold winter months, we ate almost nothing but cheese sandwiches. The Mays could not afford a water heater, so we had to boil water to take baths and wash our hair. They could not afford to give us bus money to get to school, so we had to walk miles through the snow to get to and from school each day.

The stress of the lean winter months soon frayed everyone's nerves. After a particularly meager dinner of tomato soup, I lingered at the table, playing with the tablespoon and absentmindedly bent the spoon.

When Anne saw this, she got angry. "What are you doing?" she shouted. She reached over and gave me a hard slap across the cheek. I was too stunned to react. Memories of physical abuse in the orphanage came flooding back as I fought back tears.

"Don't hit my brother!" Adriano shouted, furious. Anne's slap had sparked unpleasant memories for him as well.

Hearing all the commotion and high-pitched voices, Robert charged into the room. "Don't yell at your mother!" Robert roared.

"She's not our mother. She hit my brother!" In his rage and desire to protect me, Adriano abruptly stood and threw his chair toward Anne.

"What's going on?" Robert screamed. Adriano picked up another chair and lifted it in the air, ready to throw it at Robert, who seemed to be egging him on. Standing six feet tall, Robert towered over us and moved toward Adriano to subdue him. I had to protect my brother. I had promised my dad I would. I frantically pummeled Robert's back with my fists while shouting for him to leave Adriano alone. Bobby ran to a corner in the room. He sat there and quietly trembled while we ganged up on Robert. Anne had never seen anything like it. Sobbing, she phoned the police.

Within minutes Adriano and I were led from the house in handcuffs and pushed into the back of a patrol car. I halfheartedly hoped we would go careening through the streets with the lights flashing and siren blaring, but instead we drove quietly to Juvenile Hall, where we stayed for a week. We were not worried about Bobby. Besides being the Mays' favorite, he was such a gentle soul that the possibility of him doing anything to displease the Mays was highly unlikely.

"At least this place has hot water," Adriano said after emerging from a hot shower.

"Yeah, no kidding," I said. "This place is not so bad."

"Yeah, maybe we'll stay here forever."

"At least we don't have to eat any more cheese sandwiches!"

A week later, we reluctantly climbed into the Mays' station wagon. The icy silence in the car ride home hung almost as thick and heavy as the cold outside.

"Go to your rooms," Robert said gruffly after he unlocked the front door. Adriano and I did as we were told. We went to our rooms quietly. We were hurt.

"Aaaah! Stop hitting me!"

My eyes snapped open, and I leapt out of bed. We had been home for only a few days. I raced upstairs to find Robert whipping Adriano on his bare back with his thick leather belt. I screamed, and Robert turned around, pointing at me in anger. "One word out of you, and you're next," he said, glaring at me until I left the room.

I fled back to the basement and stayed put. Later, Adriano showed me his back. He explained to me that Robert and Anne had gotten angry with him when he refused to dust the furniture early in the day. To get back at them, he picked up some of Anne's expensive figurines and broke them by throwing them on the floor. Seeing this, Anne slapped him hard on the face, and then Robert started whipping him on the back with his belt.

Hearing this, I completely lost it. I dug out the phone number of David Ardapple, a social worker who had stopped by a few times to make sure we were adjusting to our new life in the United States.

"Hello, David speaking," the voice answered on the other end of the phone.

"Mr. Ardapple," I said, speaking quietly and quickly. "This is Fernando. You remember me?"

"Yes, of course, Fernando! How are you?"

"Well, not good, Mr. Ardapple. Mr. Mays is upstairs right now beating Adriano with a belt, beating him really bad."

"Why is that, Fernando? What's going on there?"

I quickly told him the story of the bent spoon and our stay at the Juvenile Hall. Mr. Ardapple listened in silence.

"And how is everything else going there at home?" Mr. Ardapple asked. "Do you feel safe? Do you feel you are being well cared for?"

I thought of the lack of food and hot water and the long walks we suffered to and from school each day in the freezing winter.

"Well, you see, Mr. Ardapple…."

A couple of days later, I trudged up to the Mays' house after school, absorbed in my thoughts. I almost did not notice the strangers in the kitchen talking to Anne. They stopped talking when I walked into the room. Anne put down her coffee.

"Fernando," she said stiffly. "This is Mr. and Mrs. Kuehnel. They'd like to say hello to you."

"Hi," I said awkwardly, not sure what was going on.

"Hello, Fernando!" Mrs. Kuehnel said warmly, grinning broadly at me.

"Hi, Fernando," Mr. Kuehnel said, standing up to shake my hand. "How about we take you and your brothers out for an ice cream cone?"

"Um, OK," I said, unsure why these strangers would want to take us for some ice cream. But I went along with it.

We piled into the Kuehnels' big brown van and rode to the ice cream parlor down the road. We had a pleasant time chatting with the Kuehnels. They were nice people. They asked each of us questions about ourselves, such as how we were finding school and what activities we liked to do for fun. It was a nice break from the tension-filled environment at the Mays'.

Becky Kuehnel drove her lumbering van through the streets, keeping her eyes peeled for the small figure of the boy she had met the day before. Her thoughts circled back to what she had seen at the Mays' house during her brief visit. She could sense the strain in Anne's voice from the moment she greeted them at the door. The social worker had let Anne know that Becky and Skip were coming, but it almost felt like she had been reluctant to let them in.

They had had an awkward conversation at the kitchen table while waiting for the boys to get home from school. Becky got the distinct feeling that the woman who had taken them in, the woman who was supposed to be acting as a surrogate mom, actually did not even *like* these boys.

As the boys came home one by one, the tension in the house became palpable; Anne and Robert stiffened while my brothers and I became quiet and obedient. We hardly said a word at the house, but we spoke up when Becky and Skip asked us direct questions at the ice cream parlor. As she and Skip watched us enter the Mays' house after dropping us off, Becky felt so sorry that we had to live in the tension of that home.

With several children adopted from various countries, Becky had seen and heard her share of the hardships that children have endured in orphanages. She thought that the worst thing in the world would be for us to wind up in an environment that was just as cold and unloving as the one we had escaped from.

I was listening to the snow crunching underneath my feet as I walked home from school when a van slowly pulled up beside me.

"Hey, what are you doing walking around with no jacket on? It's so cold outside!" The voice of Becky Kuehnel rang out through the icy air. "Get in. I'm going to your house."

I was stunned to see the woman I had met a day earlier. Why was she here? I climbed into the van.

"I'll take you home—well, to your old home, and your new home, too."

I looked at her in surprise.

"Oh, you're coming home with me. You and Adriano and Bobby are all going to come and live with me and my husband on our farm. Won't that be nice?"

I was speechless, my mind so tangled in confusion that I did not know what to say. Moments later, we pulled up to the Mays' house. Anne and Robert were waiting at the front door. I leapt out of the van and walked up to them with a question mark on my face.

"We don't want you anymore" was Robert's greeting as he folded his bulky arms across his massive chest.

"You tore this family apart," Anne said accusingly, dabbing her red eyes with a tissue. "You are responsible for breaking up this family."

Their words pierced a hole in my heart.

"What?! What do you mean? What are you talking about?" I said in disbelief, my eyes welling up with tears. When they turned away, I ran past them and down the basement steps, only to find the door to my room chained and locked. Long wooden planks were nailed across the door, making it impossible to enter, even though I had the key. I seethed with hurt and anger. The Mays had made it clear: I was no longer welcome in their home.

Not another rejection! Stunned thoughts raged through my tortured head as I broke down in tears, beating on my sealed bedroom door. I had been rejected by my first parents—my real, biological parents—and now I was being rejected by my second parents, too. They did not value me; they thought I was worthless…so worthless that they could just throw me away and kick me out.

Why does this keep happening to me? Am I not good enough? Why doesn't anyone want me? I crumpled onto the floor, heaving with sobs as the fresh pain of this latest rejection tore open all of my old wounds from childhood—all those nights spent wishing for my mom, all those days spent waiting for my dad. When I arrived in America, I thought I had found a new family, a family who loved me, valued me, and wanted me. But it wasn't true; it was all a lie. They *did not* want me…and now I would be tossed out like yesterday's garbage. This second rejection hurt even more than the first abandonment, like rubbing salt into a deep cut that had not yet healed.

I lay slumped against my bedroom door, trying to catch my breath as I went over the situation in my head. In just a few moments, I would be leaving the Mays' house forever. I was going to live with the Kuehnels, whom I had met just the day before. I looked up at the planks nailed firmly across my door and wondered if the Mays would let me retrieve some of my things that were trapped inside.

"Fernando, I think it's time to get going," Becky's voice called from upstairs.

I lifted myself up slowly and plodded up the stairs, using all my willpower not to scream with rage. The scene upstairs was chaotic as Bobby cried inconsolably. He rarely cried, mostly because he did not know what was happening. But seeing Adriano and me crying made him cry, too.

"Your room is sealed shut. I'm sure you noticed," Robert said.

"We took some clothes out of your room," Anne said, pointing to a lumpy plastic bag on the floor. "You can take that with you."

"But what about my art? My drawings…and my photo albums?"

"You can leave now," Robert said stiffly and sternly, motioning me toward the front door.

My brothers and I were forced to leave abruptly, without any of our most personal and prized possessions. As I hoisted the bag of clothes onto my shoulders, my mind flitted to my clock radio and the Michael Jackson records that I was so proud to have bought with my own money, using the small wage that I had earned by pedaling my bike through the icy streets the previous winter, flinging newspapers onto people's lawns, and the drywall construction jobs I did with Robert. I thought of my pencil drawing of a pitcher, the one I had labored over for many hours to make it just right. Anne had been so proud of me for that pitcher drawing that she had framed it. What went wrong? What would the Mays do with my photos and drawings? *Probably throw them away*, I thought. *Maybe they already have.*

As I walked out the front door for the last time, I made a vow that the Mays would regret kicking me out. One day I would *be* somebody. I would prove to the whole world that I was worth something, and then the Mays would realize how badly they had treated me. I would show them—one day.

The winter of 1983 was the breaking point for the Mays family. My brothers and I had to start anew, *once again*.

The Kuehnels in 1983 before we arrived. This photo was taken during the wedding of David, who is Skip and Becky's youngest biological son.

Chapter 8

The Kuehnels

As Robert firmly shut and locked the front door, Becky gave each of us a gentle hug, holding us as we cried on the front lawn.

"You have a new family now," she told us.

I was not sure what had just happened. Even though things weren't perfect at the Mays', it was the only real family experience I had ever had. I felt as worthless as the garbage I used to pick through. The words 'I don't want you' echoed through my mind like a knife blade through the heart. *What's the point of existing if no one wants you—if even your mom doesn't want you?* I wondered. As a crippling pain squeezed my chest, I wished I would just wither up and die right there on the Mays' front lawn. Anne Mays had told me that I was responsible for breaking up the family. Was it true? Was it all my fault? Was I so horrible that I caused all of this?

Becky broke my reverie by gently touching my arm. "Let's go now, Fernando," she said. I climbed into the passenger seat as my brothers jumped into the back of the van with their bags of clothes. Becky drove off as I took one last look at the house where we had lived in for the previous two years.

I was quiet as Becky navigated the van toward the highway. I went over the events in my head, trying to figure out what had just happened. When I had called Mr. Ardapple, I did not expect that it would result in our removal from the Mays' home. I did not expect my parents to suddenly not want us anymore. Things had been getting worse, but I never expected this. When had they decided I was so horrible? Was it when I brought home the beer? Was it the horrible night I'd bent the spoon and wound up in jail? In any case, I resolved that I would someday put the Mays in their place.

I turned to Becky. "Can I go to college?" I asked her intently. "Will you help me?"

Becky looked surprised to hear such ambitious words coming out of my mouth, especially after what had just happened.

"Well," she said, "We cannot afford to pay one hundred percent of your college costs, but we will do all we can to help you get ready for college when you are through with high school."

She explained that I would have to work hard if I wanted to go to college and that I would have to make really good grades. She explained that she and her husband did not have a lot of money, but she promised that they would do what they could to help me.

"OK, that's good," I said, settling back in my seat. "Thank you." I stared out the window, barely noticing the highway rolling past as I blinked back tears. *I'll become a doctor*, I thought. *Once I'm a doctor, the Mays will have to respect me.*

In the back seat, Bobby asked Adriano where we were going.

"To our new home," Bobby said. "I hope they're rich."

Two hours later, Becky pulled the van into the long driveway leading up to their farm. It was a sizable property situated around a large two-story farmhouse that was flanked by several outbuildings.

"This is your home?" I asked Becky, looking around. It was completely different from the farm where I had worked in the Philippines years earlier.

"Yes, this is where we live," she said, pulling up to the house. "That's Tyrone, Ho-Chang, and Caleb. They are your new brothers. Two of them, anyway."

An African American teenager and two Korean boys were playing basketball in the driveway.

"How many other children do you have?" I asked her.

"Well, with you three, the total is sixteen," she answered. "But most of them have grown up and left home already."

"Sixteen kids!" I exclaimed. "How many of them are adopted?"

"I don't divide up my children that way," Becky responded. "I see all of my children as my children, whether they were adopted or whether I gave birth to them. I love and care for them all equally. But to answer your question, with you, Adriano, and Bobby, we have adopted thirteen kids in total. Right now it is just the three boys staying here with us."

"Wow," I said. "Why do you adopt all these kids?" I asked quietly as she brought the van to a stop.

"Because, my son, the world needs more parents than children," she answered, turning to me with a matter-of-fact smile.

I awoke the next morning to the scent of warm pancakes wafting through the house. I sprang out of bed. It had been so long since I last had pancakes that I could barely remember what they tasted like. I threw on some clothes and dashed downstairs to the kitchen.

"Fernando, good morning!" Becky called out. "You're just in time—breakfast is nearly ready."

She bustled around in her apron, flipping pancakes and tossing them onto plates as they were ready. Skip made coffee and told me to grab a plate and pull up a chair. I joined everyone at the table and apprehensively soaked in the atmosphere, not sure what to expect with this new "family." Would they someday kick me out, too?

To my surprise, the conversation over breakfast was lively and spirited. It was a far cry from the gloomy pallor that had fallen over the Mays' house the previous few months. My new parents had a light, easygoing manner that seemed to engage the kids and help us open up. Plus, Becky's pancakes were delicious. I washed them down with a full glass of orange juice.

After breakfast, Tyrone, Ho Chang, and Caleb threw on their coats and scarves, grabbed their backpacks, and rushed off to the bus stop.

"You three won't be going to school today because we didn't get the chance to enroll you yet," Becky said to my brothers and me as we cleared the table. "We'll enroll you in school first thing today so that you can start on Monday."

"Since you'll be home today, how about we show you around the farm and get you familiar with our routine?" Skip said. "Everyone has chores to do here, so we'll show you what to do."

We helped wash and dry the dishes, then waited as Becky called the local junior high and high schools to enroll the three of us as transfer students. While she was on the phone, Skip dug up three jackets and handed them to us.

"Here you go," he said. "You'll need these for outside. We noticed you did not have any jackets. These are hand-me-downs, but they'll keep you warm."

I stepped out into the cold Wisconsin air and watched my breath turn white in the morning sun. I was snug in this new jacket; for once I could stand outside in the frigid weather and not feel the biting chill against my bones. I thought the Kuehnels were friendly and found their openness disarming, but I still felt on edge. I was not ready yet to trust them—I had been hurt too many times before. I turned around as Skip, Becky, and my brothers joined me in the yard.

"We run a veal farm here," Skip explained as they walked toward the outbuildings. "It's a family business, so everyone takes part, and everyone gets paid for their work."

"The money you make is yours to spend or save however you want," Becky added.

Skip opened the barn door and led us all inside. The smell of manure and sweaty farm animals filled the air. Stepping back for a moment, I covered my nose because the smell was so overpowering. "These are our calves," he said, gesturing toward the rows of baby cows in their pens. "We feed 'em for four months, then they get sold."

"We feed them twice a day," Becky said while getting the milk formula ready, "So that's one of the jobs here."

"We also have sheep to feed," Skip said. "Fernando, that can be your job. Let me show you where we keep the grain." He showed all three of us where the grain was kept. Bobby and Adriano also had the same job, but Skip told them that they would take turns feeding the sheep. All of us were expected to help out in the barn to feed the veal unless we had homework.

For the rest of the morning, Becky and Skip gave us a tour of their farm, showing us all the animals and explaining how they needed to be cared for. They pointed out the pasture where the animals grazed and the fields where they baled hay. Becky walked us through the garden, pointing out the various vegetables that grew in the winter.

It was a lot to take in all at once—being suddenly yanked out of my familiar world and thrown into this whole new routine, with a whole new family who had a whole new style of doing things. But I had no choice.

The thing I had learned from living on the streets is that you need to be adaptable to survive in the world, so I took on my new chores without complaint.

"We'll get you guys on the payroll starting today," Skip said. "After you finish your chores, you're free to do what you want—get acquainted with the animals, walk around the farm. Mom will call you for lunch."

"Oh, and since you're not in school tomorrow, we've set up doctor's appointments for all of you," Becky added.

"What for?" Adriano asked. "There's nothing wrong with me."

"It's just a checkup, honey," Becky said. "Have you guys had a checkup since you've been in the States?"

We shook their heads.

"I kind of thought so," Becky said. "Well, you've been here for three years, so it's about time."

Our first US doctor's visit reminded me of all the doctors we saw right before we left the Philippines, with all the poking and prodding.

I keenly paid attention to everything that happened during the visit, imagining myself someday working in that environment. It was a thorough checkup; the nurses measured our weight and height, took our temperature and blood pressure, checked our sight and hearing, drew some blood, and asked for urine samples. When the doctor arrived, I took note of everything she said and did so that I could someday emulate her words and actions with the same knowledgeable, authoritative air. I watched as she pulled out all kinds of special instruments to listen to my heartbeat and lungs and to look inside my nose, ears, and throat. She shined a light into my eyes, checked my spine, and tested my reflexes. When the exam was done, she remarked that I was in good health—except that my ears needed to be cleaned out. So did Adriano's and Bobby's.

Becky watched as the doctor inserted an instrument into our ears that flushed out the buildup of earwax and dirt. "Wow," she remarked as a flood of gross, jelly-like crud spilled from our ears. "No wonder you couldn't learn English in Green Bay," she teased. "You couldn't hear it!"

After dinner that night, I waited for the Kuehnels to go into the living room and turn on the TV, but they did no such thing. Instead they served everyone a bowl of ice cream and sat around the table, chatting with the kids. It was apparent that the Kuehnels were much more cultured and educated than the Mays; I could tell just by the way they talked and the things they talked about.

"Do you play any instruments?" Becky asked me.

"I took clarinet lessons in Green Bay," I answered.

"Ah, if you like wind instruments, we've got a trumpet you can play," she said. "We'll teach you guys music. I can lead on the piano and sing while you play. Tyrone plays the saxophone, too."

"It's the most fun around Christmas time," Tyrone chimed in. "We all sing and play Christmas carols around the piano."

"Yes, you'll enjoy that!" Becky said.

Before going to bed that night, I thanked the Kuehnels for taking my brothers and me to the doctor. I was grateful to them, yet I still felt distant, so I quickly retreated to my room for an early night.

As I lay in bed unable to sleep, my eyes burned with tears as I thought of Anne and Robert Mays. Did they miss us? Probably not. I wondered if they ever really loved us. I mean, we did have some good times with the Mays, especially with our cousins Karin, Dawn, and Matt. We had grown close to them and were forming a strong bond. Dawn was so funny, Karin was kind, and Matt was fun. *Do they miss us?* I wondered.

I thought about all the things I had to leave behind. I seethed with anger when I thought of my photo albums sitting on my old bookshelf, filled with the photographs I'd carefully mounted. I missed those pictures; they were part of me, like so many other things in my room that the Mays would not let me take. To be stripped of the few possessions I ever owned was a terrible blow. Vowing that I would one day prove my worthiness to the Mays, I fell asleep against my moist, tear-soaked pillow.

My Third Parents

I missed some of my friends at Southwest High; my departure had been so abrupt that I did not have the chance to say a proper good-bye. Yet at the same time I did not mind starting at a new school. In a way, it was like a clean slate, allowing me the chance to create a new identity. This time it was easier because my English was getting better.

I immersed myself in my studies. After returning home from school, I fed the sheep and baled the hay before sitting down to dinner. After a quick shower, my nose went straight into my textbooks. Whenever I had a question, I asked Becky and Skip for help, sensing that they were more knowledgeable than my second parents.

Becky quickly recognized my potential and drive to succeed. In the evenings, she went out of her way to drive me to extra night classes so that I could brush up on my English, which was the first step to better understanding all of my other classes. I also took extra classes in other subjects, such as algebra and trigonometry, so that I could qualify for college. Throughout my last two years of high school, my primary focus would be getting into college.

School sports became an important outlet for me. Becky and Skip allowed me to join the wrestling team, which became a way for me to channel and release my pent-up anger that had been building dangerously since childhood. On the wrestling mat, I focused all of my rage on my opponent, who would not stand a chance. It wasn't long before first-place medals lined my shelves. Every time I received a medal, I held it with satisfaction, almost wishing that the Mays could see me and see that I was *somebody*, that I was worth keeping.

At one point, my lust for winning got the better of me. The coach warned me not to do a specific move, but I did it anyway, resulting in a broken collarbone. It was painful; I had to wear a brace until it healed. I could not wrestle anymore after that, but the coach kept me around as a timekeeper.

Even though my injury kept me from the wrestling mat, in some ways I preferred to spend my afternoons in the school gym helping the wrestling team, rather than being at home with the Kuehnels too much. I liked them well enough, but at age sixteen, adjusting to yet another new family was not easy. I had suffered too much rejection and neglect throughout my life, and the scars ran deep. I did not feel lovable. Whenever Becky or Skip told me that they loved me, I simply did not believe it. For a while, I kept expecting Skip to strike one of us. At 6'5" and more than two hundred pounds, he was a fairly big, intimidating guy. But Skip and Becky never once hit us. Unlike the Mays, Skip and Becky were aware that the kids they adopted had been through a lot, so they avoided any type of action that would cause harm to us in any way.

The Kuehnels were not only more sensitive toward their children than the Mays were; they were also more involved with us. They were more observant, responsive, and in some ways, more respectful. They got to know each child's distinct personality and in turn, each child's weaknesses or flaws. They learned where each child carried hurt from the past, and they learned each child's strong points. If anything, they strove to give each child hope for the future.

In some ways, though, my brothers and I thought the Kuehnels were too strict. For most of our childhood, we had been largely unsupervised—from roaming around in the orphanages to my time on the streets—so it felt strange to suddenly be under the close watch of two new pairs of parental eyes. Even when we were at the Mays' house, we had much more independence and mobility with our free time, so after school we were either glued in front of the TV or riding bikes around the neighborhood. At the Kuehnels', we had our specific chores to do, which limited our daily leisure activities to the farm. TV was strictly off-limits, aside from special events such as the Olympics or the Super Bowl.

Sometimes when Becky and Skip went to the barn to feed the calves, my brothers and I snuck into the house to watch TV. When we'd hear Becky and Skip opening the front door, we'd quickly switch it off and act nonchalant. It never worked, though. Skip would sense something was up and stride over to the TV, placing his wide palm in front of the screen.

"Hey, the TV feels warm," he would say to us. "Do any of you know why the TV feels warm?"

My Third Parents

We would shake our heads and shrug. After this happened a few times, Skip used his electrical engineering skills to alter the TV plug so that it required an adapter to be plugged in. After that, the TV was once and for all beyond our reach.

The TV was not the only issue the Kuehnels had rules about; they also ran a firm policy of nonviolence in their house. Throughout her life, Becky had always been a peace activist, participating in peace events and promoting international relations. Several peace posters hung around the house. They always strived to instill an attitude of nonviolence into their children.

They worried about Adriano's tendency toward violent outbursts. He was often in trouble at school for getting into fights and acting out. So when he came home one day with the permission forms required to try out for football and wrestling, the Kuehnels refused to sign them. Why encourage violent behavior by allowing him to engage in violent sports? They were concerned that the competitive atmosphere of those physical games could ultimately have a detrimental effect on Adriano's behavior, further inciting his combative tendencies.

As much as they sought to keep negative traits in check, the Kuehnels also believed in rewarding good behavior. They wanted their kids to earn their rewards rather than expect everything to be handed freely to them. So before someone was allowed to try out for sports or borrow the car, he or she must first have good grades, display good behavior at home and at school, and never act aggressively. Although all of us kids sometimes saw them as strict, Becky and Skip simply wanted their kids to have fulfilling lives and reach our highest potential. Their parenting policies were always centered on helping their children function well in the real world.

Even though they had a parenting style that I was not at all used to, I liked the Kuehnels. It was obvious that Becky loved being a mom. She prepared the family meals and loved having extra people come over on weekends and birthdays. In many ways, the Kuehnel farm was like a hive of constant activity that kept the children stimulated. Tyrone played the saxophone and was in track, Ho Chang and Caleb played the trumpet.

As I flipped through one of the Kuehnels' many photo albums, I gazed at all the different faces peering out at me from the photographs. There were white faces; dark faces; tan, brown, and black faces—all living under the same roof. Becky sat next to me on the couch, telling me out everyone's names and where they were from.

In addition to all of their children, they also had provided a home to twelve foreign exchange students who had come to stay with them over the years, starting with a student from Malawi whom they hosted one summer. Some foreign exchange students stayed for a few months, while others stayed for as long as a year. Some were high school age; others were college students.

Becky pointed out pictures of all the friends they made after they started adopting. Once they decided to adopt, they started to socialize with a lot of other families who had already been through the adoption process, so they got a lot of help as they went through the process the first few times. In turn, they tried to assist other families who were going through the application process and making decisions. She showed me photos from some of their gatherings back when the families had a lot of Korean children. They got together once a week for a special Korean class where they learned about the dancing, music, and language of Korea. They had a big chart on the wall at that time with Korean words on one side and the English translation on the other so that the adults and kids were both learning foreign vocabulary at the same time. Rather than Americanize their kids, the Kuehnels always sought to honor their cultural heritage and teach the kids to be proud of where they came from.

"Maybe we should do that for you and Adriano and Bobby," Becky said. "Create a wall chart with words in Tagalog and words in English. Can you say something in Tagalog?"

I thought for a moment, but my mind stumbled over the right words. I was stunned to realize that I could not articulate my thoughts in Tagalog anymore because the Mays had forbidden us to speak Tagalog in their

My Third Parents

house. I had spent the previous few years desperately trying to learn English—so much that I had all but forgotten my native tongue. "Um, no, I don't remember much Tagalog," I mumbled, repressing my tears and anger.

"Oh, that's too bad," Becky said. "Preserving your own culture is so important."

I could not help but wonder how things might have turned out differently if Skip and Becky had been our first adoptive parents.

"It's important to get along with people who are different from you," Becky mused as we looked through her old photographs. "Cross-cultural understanding is one of the first steps for bringing about world peace."

Hearing her words, my mind flashed back to my high school cooking class that morning. Ever since I started my new school, I hated going to cooking because an ignorant kid named Al kept calling me racist names like "gook." Al never left me alone. While I sat in my seat and listened to the teacher's instructions for making pigs in a blanket, Al sat in the kitchenette across from me and slung insults at me, one after the other. I remembered Becky's admonitions about not engaging in violence, so I tried to ignore Al the best I could. Unfortunately, that just egged Al on even further until I could not take it anymore. One day when the teacher was not around, Al and I got into a fist fight, exchanging blows as the other kids shouted with excitement. I hated to disobey my newest parents, but it was worth it. Al left me alone from then on. I was in tears after the fight. Although I was used to the fighting, I hated to fight with anyone, unlike Adriano, who seemed to welcome it.

"We are glad to have you and your brothers here with us," Becky said, snapping me out of my reverie as she closed the photo album. "You bring so much to this family. We've already started the paperwork to legally adopt you, so it won't be long before you are a Kuehnel."

I felt numb at her words. I'd never been wanted by anyone in my whole life, and now my new foster mother was welcoming us with open arms. Along with the usual teenage angst and insecurity, each day of my life was a constant battle over my abandonment issues—but no one else knew about it, except maybe my brothers, who were probably feeling the same way. I quickly excused myself and said good night, pretending to be tired so that I could deal with my ongoing confusion, pain, and anger in the privacy of my bedroom.

Skip stood outside the door and listened. Through the closed door, he could hear my muffled sobs and the gentle rhythm of the rocking chair rolling slowly back and forth on the wood floor. He opened the door. Becky held me in her arms, stroking my back and patting my head. "It's OK, it's OK, Fernando," she murmured occasionally. "We're here, it's OK. We love you."

Becky and Skip had been taking turns holding me ever since my outburst that morning. They were quite taken aback. What had been a simple "I love you" on Becky's part had released an unforeseen torrent of emotion from their newly adopted son.

They could not say that they understood how I felt because that would have been a lie. But they could certainly imagine how I felt. They could sense my deep hurt from years of rejection and abandonment. In my sobs, all of the pain from my neglected childhood came pouring out. They could only hope that it was a healing release.

"I love you boys," Becky had said that morning, giving us each a hug after Skip announced that the adoption had been processed successfully. "You are now a Kuehnel!" he had said happily.

I pulled away abruptly as I processed this news. Without warning, I quietly said, "How can you say you love us if you don't even know us?"

"Pardon, Fernando?" Becky said.

"I said, 'How can you say you love us if you don't even know us?'" I repeated louder this time, almost shouting angrily. "You do not know me. You do not know what we've been through." As I said the words, they caught in my throat and turned into tears. Embarrassed at my display of emotion, I turned and ran upstairs to hide in my bedroom. I felt angry, hurt, and defiant. I had always wanted to be loved by a parent, but all those years of *not* being loved by a parent made me feel that I was simply unlovable. Even the Mays never said "I love you." I did not know how to react to the Kuehnels freely giving their love and saying those words all the time. I was angered that she could say it in such a casual and flippant way.

After a few moments, Becky and Skip followed me up the stairs and waited patiently outside my door. They could hear me crying inside. Becky slowly opened the door and quietly stepped into the room.

By the time I reached the Kuehnels, I was already sixteen years old—almost an adult. I was very aware that the other teens around me had no idea of what I'd experienced, and neither did the adults. The Kuehnels did not know my whole story; they did not know the details of my childhood or the countless nights that I had cried myself to sleep, wishing for the love of my mother and father. Yet when Becky said "I love you" to any of her adopted children, she meant it. In those three words, she was trying to let us know that she cared for us, that she would always stand by our side whenever we needed her. She knew that most of her adopted children came to her with broken wings, and it was her calling in life to help them mend and learn how to fly.

Up until that moment, she had not realized the profound effect those three words could have on her adopted children. In me, those three simple words sparked a wide range of emotions—surprise and disbelief followed by defiance and anger, which finally melted into pain as all the hurt of my childhood was flushed out. That emotional afternoon spent crying in the arms of Becky and Skip was a cathartic release for me, unraveling the memories of an unloved childhood. As I wept, I remembered all the times I had longed to hear those words, "I love you," from a parent—from *my* parents. How many times I had wished for them to hold me the way Becky was holding me now, to stroke my hair and protectively tell me that everything was going to be OK, that I was safe.

Was I safe now? I did not know. I could not fully trust it. But from that day on, I started trusting Becky and Skip. I was able to accept and "see" Becky as "Mom" and Skip as "Dad," although I still struggled to call them Mom and Dad.

All of my extra ESL evening classes and summer school classes were starting to pay off.

"Guess what, guess what!" I shouted exuberantly as I burst through the door.

"What is it?" Becky said. Skip lowered his newspaper expectantly.

"I won first place in the Voice of Democracy contest! My essay won first place!"

For the previous few weeks, I had labored intensively over my essay, searching for the right words to get my meaning across. The contest was open to everyone at Kiel High School. I knew that I had tough competition on all sides because the other kids had all been familiar with English since the day they were born, whereas I had started learning only a few years earlier.

Winning the contest was a victory for me in more ways than one. I had proven that with dedication and drive, I could rise to the top, even though I had started at the bottom. I wished that the Mays could see me now. Brimming with joy at my success, my future had never looked brighter.

My essay represented the local VFW chapter in the district contest at Green Bay. The local newspaper published the essay in its entirety:

> Today's youth are ambitious, idealistic, concerned, and highly educated. They have the creativity to build a better world, tomorrow.
>
> In the past, the ages of people who owned their own business might have been in their forties or older. Now it is not unusual for people in their teens and twenties to have a business of their own. This has become possible because of the demanding education and

the advanced technology this country offers. The young people of this country are highly motivated to learn and to help this country to be strong and to be a beautiful place to live. Not only are today's youth America's future builders, but perhaps America's youth are the future builders and helpers of the world, too.

American youth are reaching for the new horizon of brotherhood. Samantha Smith was one of the young Americans who helped promote peace between the countries of the United States and Russia or even perhaps among countries all over the globe. She wrote a letter to the leader of Russia, Yuri Andropov, and she and her family were invited to visit Russia. She was proud of the United States, and we can be proud of her.

Young American pop and rock musicians devoted their talent and time to "USA for Africa" to help the starving people. These compassionate young people are living in a democracy, which gives them freedom to help other countries that are in trouble.

The young people of America are the people who are going to accomplish what their parents had set out to do. They're going to take over what their parents started, but how and whether these plans will be accomplished depends upon the vision of American youth. They will have control of our cities, states, and nations. They will be our future leaders as well as ordinary citizens and taxpayers.

Our advancing technology will be continued by this country's younger generation. They are the people who are going to continue the research that is being conducted at this moment. They are going into the lab in the future, taking over from their parents. The future of this country relies on the hands, minds, and hearts of the young Americans.

Many people around the world wish that they could go into this country called the United States. They want to live in a free, beautiful, peaceful, and well-formed country such as this, the United States of America. Freedom relies on everyone's contributions; it does not matter how young or old you are in this country. Many people immigrate to this country; that is how much this country means to so many people. These young foreigners who came from abroad to this country will be America's future doctors, scientists, researchers, governors, and anything else they wish, just like the young people born in this country. This freedom does not discriminate because of racial background, sex, social status, or looks. This is called the country with a government of the people, by the people, for the people. That is what makes this country so unique, so respected, and so loved.

The future of this country depends upon America's youth. They are going to sit where you are sitting. You may adopt all the policies you please, but how they are carried out will depend upon America's youth. People everywhere can look forward to a bright, new tomorrow, just over the horizon, by preparing themselves today. For tomorrow will come—it always does. And with the dawn comes responsibility and opportunity. America's young people accept the challenge of carrying on the torch of freedom into a new day.

I carefully saved the newspaper page that announced my win and reproduced my essay. Winning the Voice of Democracy contest was one of my proudest achievements to date, bolstering my self-esteem. It helped me to realize that I *could* do something and be someone, and that when I spoke up, other people would take notice and listen.

The Kuehnels believed that when people turn eighteen, they become adults who can make their own decisions. In their view, at eighteen years old, people should have the maturity and sense of responsibility to make it on their own after finishing high school. As parents, they were still completely willing to provide emotional support and give parental advice long

My Third Parents

after their kids left the nest, but they did not want any of their kids to try to linger at the family house too far into adulthood.

I reached my eighteenth birthday during my senior year of high school. Due to my lonely childhood, I'd always been fiercely independent, and after two years, I still found it hard to conform to the Kuehnels' way of doing things. Because I was eighteen, I felt I should have more control over my own life, but I was still stuck in their house and locked into their routine until I graduated from high school.

One day, our differences mounted into an argument. I felt they were being too controlling, so I left home for a couple of months, staying at my friend Paul's house. I met Paul in high school. He was kind to me and was from a good Christian family. He happily offered to let me stay at his home.

I still went to school every day. One day, my guidance counselor called me into her office.

"Hi, Fernando," Mrs. Rieter said as I walked into the room. "I wanted to talk to you about your college plans. Have you started applying to colleges yet?"

"No, not yet," I said. "I've started researching them, but I haven't actually applied yet."

"Well, what are you waiting for? Now is the time. You need to apply before the deadlines pass. How about financial aid? Have your parents filled out the forms for you yet?"

"Um, no," I said meekly. "I left home a couple months ago. I have not talked to Mom and Dad much. I've been staying with a friend."

"Oh, really?" Mrs. Rieter looked at me closely. "What happened?"

"Oh, nothing bad," I said quickly. "They didn't hurt me or anything," I added, thinking back to Robert Mays whipping Adriano. "They're really nice people; I just thought I needed more freedom. They were too controlling."

Mrs. Rieter looked at me sympathetically. "Well, you're gonna need your parents' signatures on your financial aid forms," she explained. "They'll need to fill out their financial information, such as their income and assets. This is very important, or else you won't qualify for financial aid at all."

My heart sank at the news. I thought I was so ready to pave my own way in the world, but now I was being told I needed my parents' help—like it or not.

"Listen," Mrs. Rieter said, leaning forward. "I know you may have your differences with your parents, but that's common with people your age. I know you probably feel ready to strike out on your own, but you really should reconcile with your mom and dad. If you get into college, you'll be leaving in less than a year anyway, so you won't have to live with them for too long," she said with a kind smile.

"Yeah, you're right," I said. I wanted to go to college so badly that I was not going to let a silly argument with my parents stand in my way. "I'll call them after school, and I'll start applying for colleges right away."

The next day, I swallowed my pride and returned to the Kuehnel home. They welcomed me almost as if nothing had happened.

Becky kept her promise to help me get into college. I really wanted to go to medical school, but Becky advised me that I did not have the grades for it. She helped me get some information from colleges in the area. After poring over the leaflets and brochures, I decided to apply to Carroll College in Waukesha, Wisconsin, because they had a good nursing program. Perhaps after getting my nursing degree, I would then be ready to go to medical school. Plus, Carroll College wasn't too far from home, so I could still come back to visit my brothers and my parents.

As I read over Carroll College's minimum requirements for grades and SAT scores, my insecurity mounted. My grades were not spectacular, and my SAT score was even worse. Would they still accept me? What would I do if they didn't? I desperately wanted to go to college and could not imagine what I would do if I could not go.

Becky double-checked my application for spelling errors. Under the "Accomplishments" section, she made sure I mentioned that I had received a Presidential Academic Award based on all the classes I had taken in the previous two years. Thanks to night school and summer school, I had squeezed into two years what most teenagers take in all four years of high school. She also included a copy of my Voice of Democracy speech, noting that I had won the contest at my high school.

The last thing she included before sealing the envelope was a three-page letter of recommendation that she addressed to the Dean of Admissions. In the glowing letter, she described to them in great detail the force of my drive to succeed. She wrote about all the extra classes I took, in addition to working at the farm and doing extracurricular activities after school. She mentioned how my reading level jumped from a fifth- or sixth-grade level when she first met me to a twelfth-grade level in just two years. She outlined the strength of my character in the face of the lifelong obstacles I had overcome—obstacles that far surpassed what most ordinary eighteen-year-olds had gone through. She hoped the letter would have some impact when they made their decision.

I waited impatiently for weeks, anxious about my future. I knew it could go either way.

One day, a letter from Carroll College appeared in the mail. I tore it open, and my eyes blurred with tears of joy as I read the first words: "Dear Fernando: We are pleased to inform you that you have been accepted into Carroll College.:

"*Mom!*" I shouted, running out to the barn, where she was feeding the calves. "Mom, I got in! I'm going to Carroll!"

Chapter 9

College, Camp, and Love

Several months later, I stepped onto a college campus for the first time as a student. I looked around at the brick buildings and majestic oaks and breathed in the clean autumn air. I could not believe it—I was actually a college student! Going to college meant a whole new level of freedom, even better than the freedom of escaping the orphanage to live on the streets. This time, my freedom brought much more promise, and my future looked brighter than ever. I was on the road to making my dreams come true. I had come a long way from being the young boy who had to pick through garbage to survive.

I looked forward to proving myself in my classes. Judy, the admissions counselor, called me to introduce herself. She explained that they took a gamble and admitted me to their program based purely on my potential, evidenced by all my hard work and the extra classes I took throughout the few years that I had been in the United States. Judy mentioned that they were impressed with Becky's letter of recommendation, which helped make their decision to give me a chance.

That fall, I moved out of the Kuehnels' farmhouse and into the dormitory on campus. I knew how lucky I was to be going there. Without the grants and scholarships I had won, I could never have afforded the $8,000-per-year tuition, and neither could the Kuehnels. As I unpacked my things and organized my new room, I could not help but feel a hint of satisfaction as Anne and Robert Mays flashed through my mind. Neither of them had ever gone to college, so I had already achieved more than they had.

My Third Parents

I was excited about all of the new opportunities that college had to offer—not just scholastically, but also socially. Steve Gerbasi recruited me to join the Delta Rho Upsilon Fraternity. I had a nice roommate named John but was too focused on school and did not have time to hang out with him. Just like all the other young adults in my freshman class, I was thrilled about being on my own. Even though I had spent most of my life so far on my own, this time it was different. When I stepped onto the college campus, I stepped into the independence of adulthood. I was ready to start this new life—unfettered from the deprivation of my past.

"Wake up!" The pounding on the door startled me out of a deep slumber. Groggily, I reached over and looked at my clock. Class started in just seven minutes! "Are you out of bed yet?" the voice boomed from the other side of the door.

"Yeah, I'm coming!" I shouted back to my friend, struggling to get out of bed. "You go ahead, I'll be there in a sec!"

I threw on some clothes and raced out the door, barely remembering to grab my textbooks. When I got to class, I thanked Pat for making sure I was up. I liked Pat. We were the only two males majoring in nursing at Carroll College, so we hung out a lot, even though we were total opposites. We did everything together, from being lab partners to buying groceries. As Pat drove to the grocery store, I would shout at him over the heavy-metal music blaring from the car speakers. When I switched it to the classical music station instead, Pat would yell indignantly and tease me for liking "old people's music." We were quite a pair. I enjoyed Pat's company for his benevolence and his wild sense of humor. Pat and I were as different as day and night. He was thoughtful, calm, and cautious. I, on the other hand, was aggressive, impulsive, and reckless at times. But we did have one thing in common: we both loved Stark Trek. If you looked at Pat, you would think you could easily boss him around him or push him around. But Pat had a strong character. He would never back down from a fight and would always stand by a friend. He was a truly great friend to have.

My first year of college was the first time I ever felt fully alive. For the first time since I had gotten to America, I felt like I belonged somewhere. A few months after starting school, I was quickly recruited to pledge a fraternity with Nick Leroy, who would become one of my best friends and longest-term friend I ever had. It was important to me because I never had a childhood friendship I could maintain. Nick is my friend to this day. Mark Rider, Steve Gerbasi, Nick Leroy, and my other fraternity brothers helped bolster my identity by providing me with a sense of brotherhood and belonging. I regarded my frat brothers as one of the first people who helped me understand the American culture and accepted me for who I was. They helped me understand the American way, and I was thrilled to be a part of it.

After all the awkwardness and struggles of trying to fit in during high school, the pieces finally fell into place after I entered college. I acquired all of the socialization skills that I did not pick up in high school and learned more about the basics of American culture, such as how to hang with guys and with girls. College was actually fun. Before long, I was nominated for Homecoming King. Because I was outgoing and funny, I quickly made a lot of friends. I caused a ruckus when I showed up at a costume party dressed as Bamm-Bamm and won the contest for Most Original Costume.

Despite all the laughter I was able to invoke in others and all of the frivolity I enjoyed with my classmates, I always felt vaguely uneasy behind my smiling facade. Perhaps I tried so hard to be charming to overcompensate for the feelings of emptiness and worthlessness eating away at me inside.

The enlightened atmosphere of higher learning was the perfect setting for me to learn about myself and start coming to terms with my past. Through my psychology classes, I learned how to examine myself and my tendencies in a new light, which I found fascinating. Aside from one isolated incident,

I no longer had to deal with the racial slurs that used to follow me everywhere I went in high school. No one at Carroll College cared if my skin was a different color or if I spoke English in a way they were not used to. Instead, they accepted me for who I am. Through classroom discussions and hanging out with my newfound friends, I learned that my opinions mattered and that other people valued my company. College helped me realize that I could contribute something worthwhile to society.

My first year of college flew by in a happy but stressed-out blur. I enjoyed many riotous nights at drinking parties with my frat brothers, learning how to let go and have fun. I somehow managed to stay on track with my studies and my grades, earning mostly B's and C's.

By my second year, I learned to moderate my partying and began to buckle down. I joined the Student Council and the wrestling team but soon had to drop out of both because schoolwork and fraternity activities took up most of my time. I arose at 7:00 a.m. every day and crashed into bed around midnight. Most of the time, my face was buried in books.

My dream of becoming a doctor grew bigger and stronger with each passing day, yet I constantly worried that my grades were not good enough. Whenever my schoolwork overwhelmed me, I thought back to that fateful day when I was locked out of my bedroom at the Mays' house. Anger surged through my veins at the memory, strengthening my resolve to succeed, no matter what. Whenever I felt like I was too tired to study or too bogged down in work to carry on, my hostility toward the Mays spurred me onward. I desperately wanted to prove to the world that I was not a worthless child who had been rejected and ignored my entire life. I wanted everyone to recognize that I was a capable and worthy person. These frustrated thoughts often drove me to tears, fueling my motivation to reach for my highest dreams.

In my third year at college, Adriano was with the US Marines and stationed in Japan. He often wrote to me and told me how lonely he was. He told me that he would get into fights with other marines as well. At one point, he sent me money to help with my tuition. Being stuck in the barracks, he saved up quite a bit and had nowhere to spend his money.

Bobby was now in high school. He got into all sorts of problems too often. At one point, he was suspended from school because he was caught drinking rum in school! This was the beginning of his emotional deterioration.

Between schoolwork and socializing, I barely had any time to visit my family. After each holiday came and went, I received disappointed letters from Becky and Skip, saying that they had missed me at Thanksgiving dinner or some other occasion. "Why didn't you come home for the long weekend?" Becky typed in her letter. "We were hoping to see you."

I folded the letter and put it away, typing out a hurried response a few days later between study sessions. I did not know quite how to explain to the Kuehnels that I preferred to stay alone in the dorms for two or three days rather than go "home" for the holidays. The truth was, I still did not feel comfortable thinking of them as "parents" because I had been so old when they took me in. I was already sixteen years old by the time Becky picked us up in her van, and I was eighteen when I left for Carroll. Those two short years were not really long enough to see them as true parents.

I knew that Becky and Skip loved me—we had been through all that—but I felt like they did not have an *unconditional* love for me. Their love was more like a practical sort of love because they did not really understand me. I called them "Mom" and "Dad," but I still felt emotionally unable to see them as real "parents." I knew they cared about me and my brothers, and I was grateful for their help, but I did not feel the same kind of love for them that I imagined a child would have for his or her parents. I simply did not know what that kind of love felt like; the opportunity to feel that sort of emotion had been stripped away from me as a child. By the time I arrived at the Kuehnel farm, I was too old and too damaged to be able to freely feel those emotions that had been stifled since childhood. Now I was glad to be on my own again, pursuing my own destiny.

As much as I preferred to stay away, I had to admit that on the few occasions when I did go home, we had a good time together. Becky would make strawberry shortcakes and do my laundry while I talked to Skip about my classes. In some way, it was easier for me to relate to them now that I was out of their house.

I lay my head on the pillow, absorbing the sounds of classical music floating around the bedroom in a strange harmony with the flickering red strobe lights. A beautiful blond girl slept soundly under my arm. I gently stroked her hair. At three and a half months, this was the longest and most beautiful relationship I had ever been in. I had the feeling that Rachel was different than the other girls I had dated in the past. When it came to Rachel, I was not just hormonally driven; I truly loved her. She was my rock, a pillar of strength. A good listener, Rachel had a soothing effect on me. She helped me calm down when I was angry or frustrated. Being the oldest of three siblings, Rachel was very caring and almost motherly. I relished the feeling of sharing intimacy with another person—something I had longed for all my life but had never found.

I had plenty of friends and enjoyed my classes. I had a promising career ahead of me and a lovely girl by my side. Yet my past shadowed me. I still found myself wondering about the mother who abandoned me in Project 8. Tears spilled down my cheeks as I wondered about my first mother, the one who had given birth to me. I longed to know who she was and why she did it. Where was she? Would I ever see her again? Despite the pain she caused when she walked away, I still wished I could see her and speak to her. I was glad that Rachel was sleeping so that she would not see me crying.

Before Rachel drifted off to sleep, she had encouraged me to start journaling about my lost mother and my childhood. "It'll help you sort out your thoughts and feelings," she had said. So as she slept, I picked up his pen and began to write, funneling my torrential stream of thoughts onto the crisp, lined paper.

Lying in bed next to Rachel's warm body, I contemplated the soothing nature of physical touch and the sense of security that goes along with it. I was six when my mom and dad abandoned me and my brothers, so at least I got six years of contact with them before they disappeared. Adriano had gotten only four, and Bobby had been the most deprived, with only two years of contact with them. "How has this affected our feelings about ourselves?" I scribbled furiously in my journal. I knew that the abandonment and the agonizing years that followed had left an indelible mark on my psyche, but I was only just beginning to scratch the surface of self-understanding. It would be a long, hard battle before I could unravel the pain and confusion that coiled tightly around my heart.

I treasured Rachel and our relationship. For the first time, I felt like I was sharing real love with someone. This was not puppy love or an obsessive infatuation; it was real love. I was sure of that, although many times she left me perplexed. She was like a puzzle I could not figure out. She was very sweet, but sometimes she was so reserved that she just seemed cold. She hardly ever showed her emotions, which I found unsettling. I was the complete opposite; I always allowed my emotions full display, even if I was feeling fiery or temperamental. I thrived on emotional expression and longed for more responsiveness from my beloved girlfriend. There were so many times when I wondered what she was thinking or feeling, but she was too hard to read. It was taking time, but with coaxing and encouragement over the previous few months, she was slowly starting to come out of her shell. I knew that she was trying, and I appreciated her for that. It was not often that people went out of their way to please me, so when she did, I cherished her with all my heart.

I slammed down the phone, fuming with anger at Becky. A half hour earlier, I had decided that a short break from studying would help clear my head, so I picked up the phone and called home to say hello. I almost wished I had not. I was shaking with fury. I swiftly grabbed my car keys and hurried over to Rachel's dorm to vent some of my rage. Maybe she would listen and understand.

Rachel opened the door, surprised to see me. "Hi, Fernando," she said. "I wasn't expecting—"

"I need to talk to you, Rachel," I said, walking past her into her room. I sat down on her bed and struggled to hold back tears. "I hate my mom. I can't believe how they're treating my brother!"

"What happened?" Rachel asked, alarmed.

I explained the Kuehnels' policy of expecting their kids to leave home and go into the "real world" on their own once they turned eighteen. Bobby had recently turned eighteen, so he was now out on his own. It was his time to make it for himself in the world. However, his childhood had been so traumatic that he was not capable of dealing with the real world, so he kept bouncing in and out of the Kuehnels' home. His life was going nowhere fast, but the Kuehnels would not step in to help, even though they claimed to "love" him.

"The other day Bobby, called Mom and asked for help," I told Rachel. "Bobby said he was hungry and wanted to come home, but Mom and Dad refused to let him come back to their house."

"That sounds like tough love," Rachel said.

I looked at her. "Tough love?"

"It's a phrase that means you might love someone, but you feel you need to be strict or firm with them because it's for their own good," she explained. "It'll help the person grow. Maybe your parents are trying to help Bobby get on his feet by making him learn to rely on himself."

I could not believe it. It felt like Rachel was taking my parents' side! I did not understand this tactic of tough love, especially because our entire childhoods had been extremely tough and completely without love. I thought back to when I was nine years old and living on the streets—now, that was tough. I knew all too well what it felt like to be hungry and lonely. It pained me to know that was exactly how my baby brother was feeling now. I was furious with Becky for not taking in Bobby during his time of need.

I got up. "I gotta go," I said abruptly, rushing out of the room before I boiled over.

Alone in my car, angry tears fought their way to the surface as I gunned the engine. I wiped my cheeks and drove blindly to the grocery store, where I threw nonperishable foods into my shopping cart, grabbing crackers and peanut butter off the shelves. I thought of packing them up in my own room, but something made me head back to Rachel's dorm.

"Are you OK?" Rachel asked when she opened the door. She let me in.

"I need to send this food to my brother," I said.

Rachel helped me pack the food in a box and tape it shut. I tried to explain why I was angry with her, but every time I tried to express what was going on inside of me, I could feel the tears welling up dangerously behind my eyes. I could not let myself cry in front of her, just like I had refused to cry when I had ridden the train from Pasay City to the duck farm as a child.

"It's OK," Rachel said. "You can explain it to me later." She could sense that this was an extremely sensitive subject, so she did not push it. As she drove to the post office, I stole a sideways glance at her profile. *I shouldn't be too hard on her*, I thought. *She does genuinely care about my feelings.* My love for her broke through my wall of pain. I did not know how she managed to be so patient with me all the time, but I was grateful that she was.

A week later, I received a letter from Bobby expressing his gratitude that someone still loved him. I felt satisfied with my good deed. Days later, another letter arrived. Bobby was requesting more help. As I put down the letter with a sigh of exasperation, I suddenly realized how the Kuehnels must have felt. I could not continue helping my brother because I had my own worries and responsibilities to deal with. Bobby was not a kid anymore; he needed to start taking care of himself. I decided to tell him so.

This time, instead of sending Bobby another care package, I wrote him a rather harsh letter. As I wrote it, I was shocked by how much the words flowing onto the paper sounded so much like the authoritarian lectures we had received from Becky and Skip. My heart ached for my lonely, lost brother, but I felt like it was time for Bobby to start pushing himself onto his feet. I did not want to do the pushing for him anymore.

A few weeks later, I went home to visit my parents. I was no longer angry with them about Bobby now that I had seen their point of view.

The house was empty and quiet with all the kids gone. Bobby had been the last one to leave. While Skip was outside working, Becky and I sat on the couch and talked. To my surprise, the conversation lasted for hours and went far deeper than we normally went.

As soon as she said, "How are you?" all of my daily worries came flooding out—anxiety about my classes, my grades, my career path, my relationship, my future. I felt like everything in the world was weighing on me.

"What do you think is causing you to feel so anxious about these things?" she asked, sipping her tea.

I reflected for a moment. When I opened my mouth, a torrent of emotional words gushed forth.

"I just feel this overwhelming pressure to succeed—to make something of my life. All my life I have felt worthless. First my real parents abandoned us, then the Mays dumped us. It's like none of them thought I was worth keeping—not even worth knowing. I want to prove to them that I am worthy and that I do deserve love. I need to prove it to myself, too. So I work like crazy and I worry like crazy, just so I can prove myself. I do not know if I can make it, but I cannot give up. I have to make it."

"Well, you know we love you," Becky said. "You don't have to prove a thing to us. We already know how wonderful you are. We love you just the way you are."

"Yeah, that's what you say...." My voice trailed off as my critical eye turned toward Becky and Skip. It was time for me to tell her how I really felt.

"You say you love us, but sometimes I don't feel it from you," I said. "You're not emotional toward us. Sometimes you almost seem cold, in some way. I mean, you say you love us, but it's not like a warm, emotional love."

I struggled to find the right words to explain while Becky listened in silence.

"You know, if someone's your mom, you expect them to show more emotion toward you. To show pain if you get into a fight or joy when you make up again. I was so mad by the way you treated Bobby when he needed help. You seemed cold, like you didn't really care."

There—I had said it.

Becky sighed. "Fernando, let me tell you a story," she began, rearranging the blanket that lay across her legs. "One of the first children I adopted was a girl named Maria. She was from Korea. A beautiful child. I welcomed her with open arms. I was so eager to let her into our lives. Then there was a crisis, and I nearly had an emotional breakdown. I couldn't speak for a whole week—and you know how much I love to talk," she said with a faint but sad smile. "I learned the hard way that I needed to place barriers to protect my own emotional well-being. I realized that most of the kids I was taking in were already damaged in some way—many of them beyond repair. Even though I loved them as if they were my own, that would never be enough to erase the years of hardship that these kids went through. After the incident with Maria, I had to back up and put away my emotions like Skip had done at the time."

I listened to her words. There was no denying the pain in her moist, bloodshot eyes. As she spoke, I recognized a lot of myself in what she was saying, and I was just one of her children. I slowly realized how patient she was to have gone through that with sixteen kids.

"I see what you're saying," I said. "I know it was hard for you sometimes. But I think you should know that your stoic attitude ends up hurting your other kids. You know, like that time Adriano left, you were hurt but you did not show it. After he came back, you did not show that you had been hurt, but you did not act too happy to see him, either. He said he felt like he was staying at a boarding house, the way you were talking to him. He felt like you didn't care. We always thought that someone who loved us like a real mom would have a more emotional reaction to us, a more positive reaction."

Becky listened quietly while I spoke. She seemed to sense my pain. She knew that I, like all the other children she adopted, had suffered greatly throughout my young life in ways that she could hardly imagine. She said she was grateful for this heart-to-heart conversation because it was bringing us closer to understanding each other. I connected more with Becky and Skip than most of the other children they had adopted. She said she did not know whether it was my maturity, my intelligence, or my desire for insight, but she knew that I was trying to reach out and connect on more than just a superficial level, and she was more than happy to reciprocate. She might not be able to soothe all the pains her children suffered, but she did want us to know that she cared.

"You know, I did feel glad that Adriano came back," Becky said, choosing her words carefully. "It was good to see him. But I guess I held back my emotions because I didn't want to show weakness to my child. I've been hurt before when I've shown my weakness."

"When you hold back like that, it comes across as arrogant," I countered. "We don't know any better if you don't tell us—we need you to show us how you feel."

I was softened by the gentle sadness that shone in Becky's eyes as the evening sun reclined, bathing the room in a golden orange light before fading into a deep blue twilight. I learned a lot about my mother that day. I used to think she was almost inhuman, but our conversation changed my mind. I was now slowly beginning to get an insight into her stoicism and her emotional reserve.

Later that night, I flipped open my journal. On its lined pages, I wrote a poem that I dedicated to Becky for having a big enough heart to sacrifice her time for so many needy children.

She stood still beside me

Her dark hair covered with silver lines,
Lines of golden age.
Eyes surrounded by roots of wisdom,

Rage grown with time and children.
Sandpaper hand she put to grind
That no one else could see.
Yet, she stood still beside me.

I ache for embrace
And she touched my soul with grace.
I struggled to be free
And stepped on a thorn.
Yet, she stood still beside me.

My sorrowed tears began to fall
And she carried me with it all.
Anger and rage, it was in me
A blinding fire to thee.
Finally, she stood still beside me.

I spoke to pierce thee,
A devil's poison snake
That can slice a man to break
I could not be a son?
She stood beside me.

My brothers and sisters demand her soul,
Spirit and all.
No time to pray for her own.
Yet, she answered all their calls
But mother stood beside them all.

I slumped against the hard plastic Laundromat chair, watching my clothes tumble inside the washing machine in rhythm with the nonstop thoughts circulating through my weary head. My T-shirt clung to my chest as the hot, humid air caused sweat to drip down my neck. *Only one more final to go—then I'll be a happy man*, I thought sluggishly as the May heat pressed in on me from all sides.

It was the end of my third year at Carroll College, and the thrill of summer loomed just over the horizon, so close I could almost taste it. I relished the feeling of release and fulfillment that always accompanied the end of the school year. I had spent the previous nine months fighting on the mental and emotional battlefield of classes and work and somehow survived. As much as I enjoyed the end of the school year, I knew that by the end of the lazy summer, I'd be ready to tackle the battlefield once more.

Thoughts of the future swirled through my tired head. I was not sure which direction to pursue as so many ideas, goals, and possible paths unfolded in my mind. All I knew was that I wanted to succeed. As the machine rinsed and spun my clothes, I fantasized about my future career. I pondered joining the Peace Corps. Fulfillment, meaning, and excitement were the three most important factors I sought in my future work. I felt like the best way to get that would be to help people who were in need. I knew too well how it felt to be in need, so I was often sickened by the self-absorbed consumerism that defined American society. When I saw people at the food court throwing away half-eaten bags of French fries, I thought of how at one time, finding a few fries in the trash would have been the night's biggest treasure for me.

At that moment, I wished I could leap into my future right away—just join the Peace Corps and be off. I wanted to see the world and other cultures, which would help me see myself differently and understand myself better. I longed to see the Philippines again and relearn my native language. But the thought of leaving behind my brothers; my lovely girlfriend, Rachel; and my family and friends held me back from doing anything so spontaneous. If I stuck around for a while, I could be a nurse or study to be a doctor or psychologist. Those jobs held meaning, too.

Fernando Kuehnel

As I cleaned out my dorm room before leaving for the summer, I discovered a few dusty boxes tucked away in the back of my closet. I pulled them out and peered inside. Amid the clutter, I found an old photo album that was taken at the orphanage. I flipped through the pages slowly and gazed at the photos of my younger brothers. Bobby looked so young in them. I studied Bobby's vulnerable smile and wondered what he was going to do with his life. I looked at Adriano's pictures and felt sorry that we seemed to be drifting apart.

I missed my brothers. We had gone through so much together—our bond was cemented until the end of time. We had depended on each other so much in the orphanage, but now all three of us were on our own. I wondered whether they were lonely and whether they ever thought of me. I worried about my baby brother, Bobby, the most, because he had suffered so much misery in his early life. *I hope he finds what he is looking for,* I thought as I sighed and packed away the photo album. *I have to learn to let go. I can't be a father to him all his life. His fate is up to him. I have to learn to take care of myself first.*

"It's coming to get you!" I shouted as the kids ran away giggling. My remote-control car bounced along the bumpy grass as I steered it toward a group of shrieking children.

"Fernando, I wrote you a poem!" a fifteen-year-old girl said. She slid up to me and handed me a folded piece of paper. "I hope you like it!" She laughed and ran off.

I was the biggest kid at camp—at least that is what my fellow camp counselors said.

Every summer since I had started college, I worked as an assistant nurse at a YMCA summer camp in Burlington, looking after boys and girls between seven and eighteen years old.

I loved summer camp because it gave me the opportunity to belatedly be a carefree child. I got along well with the kids, and they liked me, too. They were so full of energy and excitement that I wanted to run around and be a kid forever.

The high-spirited, carefree attitude of the young campers was the sweet elixir that soothed my soul, healing some of the lingering pains of my traumatic childhood. For the first time in my life, I was free to laugh and play and find amusement in all the things that kids do. When they held dances for the campers and counselors, I always had kids lining up to dance with me. They gave me the sense of recognition and belonging that I never received when I was younger, which lifted my spirits and self-esteem.

At night while the children ran around the campfire, I sat with my notebook and absorbed the atmosphere. As the children shouted and the fire crackled, I enshrined my camp experiences in a poem:

The Voices of God

The chippering sound of cardinal and sparrow
The applauding cheer of the leaves,
The whistling music of the wind.
And crushing sound of water in the lake;
Is a music symphony of the heavens.

At night, a fiesta of bellowing frogs,
The high pitch and itching of the crickets,
And the freedom call of coons in the fog;
Is the bedtime story of the spirits.

The endless echoes of young voices,
Both high and low,
The varied laughters and joy,
The crackling of leaves
That permeates to my soul,
And the little foot impressions
On the morning dew—
It is the rainbow of God's creation.

As the long, lazy summer rolled to an end, I waited near the front entrance of the deserted camp. The kids and counselors had all left earlier that day after the closing ceremony. One by one, they were picked up by their parents until only the kitchen staff and I were left. My parents were late to pick me up. I could not recall when they had ever actually showed up on time.

Now that camp was over, I felt a sense of emptiness mingled with anticipation. I did not really miss anyone in particular, although the children's smiles lingered in my memory, and their endearing remarks left a glow in my heart. I'd said a heartfelt good-bye to everyone I had come to know, but now it was time to get back to my real life.

As I waited under the hot sun, my thoughts strayed over to Rachel. I missed her. I had broken up with her at the beginning of camp because three months apart seemed like an unbearable eternity. My hormones spurred me onward; I wanted to pursue other girls without hurting her. Despite all of the flirting and kissing, none of the other girls I met at camp that summer stood up to what I'd had with Rachel. In the grand scheme of things, my summer flings seemed practically meaningless. I missed Rachel's dimples and her golden hair. I smiled wistfully at the thought of her gentle touch that could stir a wilting rose back into full bloom.

It was not the first time we had split up. I had broken up with Rachel many times since we had started dating, but I was not sure why. My feelings continuously fluctuated. Sometimes I wanted to be free, but at the same time I feared the loneliness of being single. The prospect of loss was simply unbearable. After losing so much in life, I thought I should be used to it, but that was not the case. Whenever I broke up with her, I was simply trying to spare myself the future pain of possible abandonment.

I knew that the roller coaster of our on-again, off-again relationship sent Rachel into an emotional tailspin every time I changed my mind, but I could not help it. It's not that I was wishy-washy or deliberately hurtful; it was just that I'd never once had emotional stability in all of my life. No one had ever shown me a stable, steady kind of love; I had never received a constant stream of affection from anyone. Since childhood, I'd gotten used to the turbulent emotions of being alone in an uncaring world. I had never had the opportunity to learn about giving and receiving love because so much of my early life revolved around simply trying to survive. After I got to the United States, I spent all of my time and energy learning how to fit in, adapting to a foreign culture. It wasn't until then, in my early twenties, that I finally got to experience the luxury of sharing love and enjoying life with others. It was a momentous learning experience, and it was only natural that I would make mistakes along the way.

I certainly learned a lot that summer at camp. It had been full of drama, spanning from moments of hate and anger to times of love and compassion. The few romantic flings I had led to the worst moments, helping me realize that I needed to be more cautious and selective before pursuing a girl. I learned that just because a girl was attractive did not mean I needed her in my bed.

On the flip side, I enjoyed the leisure time that came with being an assistant nurse at camp. I needed to tend to the kids only when they needed me—when they were homesick or when they sprained their ankles chasing after kids who had stolen their underwear. Between pursuing girls and handing out Children's Tylenol, I had plenty of time for socializing with the other counselors and reflecting on life. I gained insight into human nature and relationships, and I identified aspects of my own behavior that I'd never consciously noticed before. I felt like I had a long way to go before I fully explored the depths of myself, but as time went on, I felt better equipped to handle whatever challenges may lie ahead.

All in all, the previous summer expanded my perception about people and helped me become more relaxed about my problems. *I really should try not to worry so much*, I thought.

Becky and Skip pulled up the dusty dirt road in their van, interrupting my introspection. I hopped aboard the van, said an unsentimental goodbye to camp, and focused my thoughts toward the next phase of my life.

I closed my weary eyes and rested my head on my textbook. My head throbbed from too much studying. My mind drifted toward my last conversation with Becky. We had spent a couple of hours on the phone recently discussing Adriano and Bobby, who were both struggling to pull their lives together. I was exhausted; I did not know what to think or do.

For a while, Adriano had been doing all right for himself. After high school, he got into the Marine Corps, but after four years, he was kicked out. Becky said he had been discharged due to a personality disorder, but Adriano told a different story. I pieced together the fragments I had heard from Adriano and Becky to try to get the full story. It sounded like Adriano's sergeant and his company picked on him frequently, which led to a lot of fights. Somewhere along the line, the Marine Corps talked to the Kuehnels about the problem. I was not sure what was said, but I suspected that they did not have anything favorable to say about Adriano's problems. After Adriano heard that the Kuehnels talked to the military about him, he blamed them for his discharge.

I was sorry to hear about Adriano's discharge; I knew how much the Marine Corps meant to him. I was so used to feeling responsible for my brothers that I felt inexplicably wracked with guilt, even though there was nothing I could have done in reality to prevent my brother's discharge.

Maybe I could have been more supportive of Adriano throughout the years, I wondered miserably. *What if my impatient attitude toward him helped wreck his self-esteem?*

Adriano was not the only one I worried about.

"By the way, Bobby is angry at you," Adriano said casually over the phone one day.

"What? Why?" I asked. I had not talked to Bobby in a while, so why should he be mad about anything?

"He thinks you don't care about him," Adriano answered. "You're never around anymore."

But I'm so busy trying to survive, I thought. *I can't take care of Bobby, too.*

Bobby wanted to continue his education, but he lost his chance. He never applied himself as a student, so his report cards were always littered with bad grades. No college would take him due to his poor transcripts. An education would have helped him have a shot at a normal life, but he blew it. I felt terrible, even though I could not be blamed for Bobby's lack of motivation and discipline.

As my eyes grew misty with tears, I remembered little Bobby at the orphanage, dependent on me for nearly everything. The three of us had been so close when we were in the orphanages together, relying on each other and protecting each other from harm. Even though we were drifting apart with age, I still loved them with all my heart. I wished we could be together again, but first I had to get my own life in order. I had to take care of myself before I could be a good influence on anyone else.

I remembered little Bobby crawling into my bed at night, as soon as he was old enough to move out of the nursery. "I'm scared," he used to whisper, his small body trembling next to me in the dark. My heart softened as my mind flashed back to our abysmally lonesome days at the orphanage. I resolved to be more lenient with my brothers. From now on, I would approach them with more sensitivity and not judge them so quickly. I hoped that someday they would be able to understand themselves better, to experience life from a healthier perspective. Only then would their insecurities fall away.

I imagined everything I wished I could tell Bobby. I knew it was too difficult to explain these things in a conversation, so I wrote them down in a poem. As I wrote, I thought of all the other neglected and abandoned children in the world, lost on the streets, looking for their moms but never finding them. What could I say to them to provide them comfort and help them through the long, sleepless nights? I yearned to tell them that there was still hope. I wanted them to know that there were ways to channel their hate and anger in a positive way. I wanted them to know that they were worthy human beings, and that they, too, could make a special contribution to the world. I wanted them to know that they mattered.

I wrote down a poem by Virginia Satir called 'My Declaration of Self-Esteem' and mailed it to Becky. "Could you please share this with

Bobby the next time you see him?" I wrote. "Maybe it will help him accept himself."

A few weeks later, I got the chance to spend a weekend with my brothers. I could sense that Adriano was starving for love; he needed someone to care for in the same way a drowning man needs a life raft. I understood how Adriano felt; it was a need for affection and love that was so strong that he would be willing to sacrifice everything to get it. I had felt that way so many times throughout my life that I recognized the signs right away. Bobby, on the other hand, was becoming more and more withdrawn, exhibiting signs of emotional dysfunction. The psychologists were starting to suspect schizophrenia.

I drove back to Carroll, burning with anger that my brothers had to suffer that kind of pain. I wished I could help them somehow, but there was nothing I could do. I had to let them go through it themselves and gain their own insights.

I hope that someday they find peace within themselves, I thought as I pulled my car into the parking lot of my dorm. *Maybe someday I'll find it, too.*

As a senior in college, my life was centered on books, work, and occasional social interaction. Most of the guys from my early years of college had dropped out or transferred, so I did not know that many people at school anymore. I thought it was better that way because it meant fewer distractions—even though it also meant many lonely nights. At least I had Rachel for comfort—when we were a couple, that is. I still kept changing my mind about our status.

My daily thoughts were dominated by my dream of becoming a doctor. To accomplish this goal, I needed good grades. I would not let anything stand in my way, including relationships. The only problem was that I was not sure exactly how to pursue my ambition. Now that I was steps away from achieving my nursing degree, I worried that it was not good enough. I had always wanted to be a *doctor*, not a nurse. However, to pay my bills and repay my student loans, I would need to take a nursing job soon after graduation. Would I be letting myself down if I just became a nurse instead? Could I ever achieve my real dream?

I assessed my main goals in life: to help others and to work in a satisfying career that would grant me the recognition I never received as a child. Becoming a successful doctor would fulfill both of those needs, but being a run-of-the-mill nurse would not. As a well-educated doctor, I would finally be respected, but more importantly, I would be needed. Everyone would look up to me and seek me out for help, even the nurses. I would be able to help my patients and at the same time help myself. *Who would have thought that a lowly street kid could someday rise above his poverty and become a doctor?* I thought.

That November, my twenty-third birthday came and went amid a flurry of classes, work, and exams. I did not have time to celebrate, but I did not feel like it anyway. The memories of all my lonely birthdays in the orphanages were enough to dampen any desire to commemorate the occasion.

When Christmas approached, I stared glumly at the meager numbers on my bank statement. I could not afford to buy presents for anyone. It reminded me of all the giftless Christmases I'd spent in the Philippines, pining for my parents. The only Christmas present I ever received was a single apple one year at the first orphanage, which I devoured in seconds flat as soon as I had it in my hands, core and all. At the time, that shiny red apple was the greatest gift in the world.

On Christmas Eve, I sat at Becky and Skip's kitchen table while everyone slept. With a pencil in my hand, I studied the smiling photographs of Becky and Skip and carefully drew their portraits on plain white paper. I meticulously outlined their features, striving to get their eyes and mouths just right, then diligently worked on the shading to make their faces look as realistic as possible. As the first light of Christmas morning filtered through the kitchen windows, I put the finishing touches on the drawings.

"Fernando, you're still up!" Becky exclaimed as she entered the kitchen, still in her bathrobe.

"Merry Christmas, Mom and Dad!" I said, presenting them their hand-drawn portraits.

"Oh wow, look at that!" Skip smiled broadly, taking a closer look. "You're good!"

"These are beautiful!" Becky said as tears came to her eyes. "You are so talented, Fernando. What a lovely gift."

"We'll get these framed and hang them right away," Skip added.

I smiled. If I had been given the chance earlier in life, perhaps I could have become an artist.

The first three years of college had felt like a battleground, but my senior year was the toughest battle of them all. There were times when I did not know if I could make it. After a full day of classes and a long shift at work, I'd collapse across my bed like a fallen soldier, waiting for unconsciousness to overcome my exhausted mind.

I'd hover on the verge of sleep before remembering a large assignment that was due or an important exam the next day. For a few minutes, I'd struggle to rise from my comfortable position, halfheartedly fighting the seduction of sleep's sweet embrace.

Then the image of Robert and Anne Mays would flash into my mind. I'd feel the crunch of snow underneath my feet as Becky slowly stopped her van beside me. I remembered the wooden planks nailed tightly across my door. *"We don't want you anymore."* Anne's words echoed in my head while Robert stood with his arms folded across his chest. Their glaring faces stared down at me while the sting of rejection shot an agonizing pain throughout my veins.

The chilling memories of that fateful day were enough to wake me up. I was not ready to admit defeat. I would fight my way to the top to ensure that the tears I spilled over the Mays' rejection were not in vain. *You'll see—you'll be sorry that you got rid of me,* I thought, clenching my teeth as I plopped myself down at my desk and opened a textbook. *I will prove that I'm better than you think I am.*

I was always surprised at how strongly these memories came back to me in moments of exhaustion and weakness. I had cried so much after they kicked me out; before that, I had been depressed, but they never acknowledged it. Toward the end, they ignored my presence, as if I was a stranger in their home. I'd felt like dying then.

With tears running from my tired eyes, the memories of being rejected by my real parents and then by the Mays flooded my heavy mind, mingling with recollections of the endless lonely nights in the orphanages and on the streets. Before I could concentrate on my studies, I had to purge myself of the painful memories that seized me in their merciless grip. My journal was my respite; writing poems saved my soul. I poured my heart into my journal, penning poems to release my wrath, calm my anxiety, and soothe my tattered heart.

> He is a child
> Innocent of his surroundings
> He does not know his existence,
> He walks where wind pushed him.
>
> His mother is not here,
> But she is in his mind
> He cries for her to come out,
> He prays for her to speak
> He listens into the wind for her voice.
> He heard nothing but his own teardrops.
>
> At night he curls into a ball
> Pretending someone is giving him a hug.
> He squeezed his pillow
> Onto his chest

As he dreams that his
Mother is next to him.
He pulls his blanket over
Him like Daddy is
Protecting him.

A young brother comes
At midnight to sleep
With him.
He becomes his mother
And a blanket to him.
They hugged each other to sleep.
Tears run down his cheeks
Down his brother's head.
As he hears his brother
Ask for their mother.

At times like these, I got so wrapped up in the inescapable pains of my past that I lost sight of how far I had risen since those tumultuous times. For a forgotten orphan from an impoverished country to now be a senior in an American college, about to graduate with a practical degree in nursing, was a genuine success. I had worked hard to get there, but I rarely gave myself credit for it. I simply pushed myself to work harder.

In the beginning of April, just weeks before graduation, my world came tumbling down in a way I'd never expected: Rachel broke up with me.

I trudged unsteadily back to my apartment as anguish ravaged my soul, ripping my entire sense of self into millions of scattered pieces. Throughout our two-year relationship, she had always been the stable one while I wavered back and forth about what I wanted. She was the solid anchor that held us together as the storm of my emotions threatened to destroy everything in sight. For Rachel to declare us finished was fatal.

The breakup was an unforeseen blow that knocked me off my feet at the absolute worst time—when I was studying for finals and scrambling to finish critical assignments. How could I carry on without Rachel?

In the months before we broke up, I had constantly worried that being in a relationship would stand in the way of my career goals. I didn't yet know how to balance my emotions with practicality. As a child, I was forced to set aside my emotions to survive, yet I never fully succeeded. Emotions only brought pain; they were almost an impediment to survival. Yet I could not deny them; they were too strong. Emotional expression was too entwined in my basic character. Now that I'd found someone to love, I feared solitude more than ever. I did not want to relive those sleepless nights crying alone in the orphanages. Without Rachel, I was lost.

Choking back tears, my mind rummaged through everything that had happened the previous few months to see if I could figure out when, where, and why our relationship fell apart. I could not help but blame myself. Rachel found someone more stable than I was. I was too focused on myself and on wanting to make it through college.

As a young man full of dreams at the start of my senior year, the world had seemed bright with opportunities. I was eager to take chances and accept sacrifices if that would lead to greater rewards down the road. Perhaps when it came to Rachel, I had expected her to sacrifice too much. Maybe she could not compromise her emotions like I tried to do. Or maybe we had just drifted apart. With my head constantly in his books or work, we hardly saw each other anymore. The previous few months had wavered between moments of loneliness and times of togetherness as we each juggled classes, jobs, and time with each other. Even when we were together, my mind was often elsewhere. But I wasn't ready to let her go.

Love was a confusing, elusive mystery that always danced just beyond reach. My heart ached to love and be loved, yet I hesitated on the brink of giving my heart fully. I could not do it. I was afraid. The fear of being hurt, of placing my trust in the wrong person, held me back. My heart had been trampled too many times before.

For the next week, I could not eat or sleep. I showed up for classes with dark circles under my eyes but pretended that nothing was wrong. I trudged through my studies like a zombie. My heart was mourning.

How can we make this work? I wracked my brain as the black letters in my textbook blurred from my tears. *How can I convince her to try one more time?*

I lowered my head into my hands and sobbed as the tears dropped onto my notebook, splotching the ink in large round circles. I missed Rachel. Even though things were not perfect, I had given a lot of myself to the relationship, and it would be difficult to get it all back.

After a few weeks of listless wandering in a heartbroken fog, a tiny slice of clarity began to emerge. I lifted my head and realized that life was continuing as normal, with or without Rachel. Either way, I would survive.

As the pain subsided, I was able to examine what I had learned from my relationship with Rachel. I had learned that sex was not a substitute for love. All of my previous sexual experiences felt empty compared to what I shared with Rachel. Through Rachel, I learned to control my childish needs, to handle my anger and curb my frustrations. I grew a lot as a person, becoming more patient with myself and with others. Most importantly, I learned that I was capable of loving and being loved.

The heartbreak taught me that I could not be dependent on anyone else's love to help me through life. My first heartbreak, when my parents left me, caused immeasurable suffering and damage, yet it did not destroy me. While the pain and loneliness from my past still resonated, I always managed to enjoy and appreciate the wonders of life. I was not about to let this breakup with Rachel destroy me.

In my journal, I tallied up my positive attributes and acknowledged that I had already accomplished a great deal in life. *I'm good-looking, caring, gentle, considerate to others…,"* I scribbled. *"Someday I'll be successful. I will not let this rejection bring me to my knees, but instead I will let it give me strength to stand on my feet again. I will continue to tread the path of life with smiles, optimism, and kindness to my fellow men. I will forgive those who brought pain to my life."*

I closed my journal and vowed to get my life back in order. I straightened out my priorities, putting girls and relationships way down the list. Instead, I would focus on my career and my dreams on the future.

It was easier said than done.

On May 19, 1991, I held a diploma in my hands. I studied the shiny gold letters that spelled my name across the paper—proof that I had survived the past four years of academic rigor and emerged victorious. All the long nights of studying had finally paid off. Carroll College had taken a gamble by letting me in, and on that day I had clearly demonstrated that they had made the right decision. *I did it! I have a bachelor of science in nursing,* I thought while everyone around me celebrated. *So why don't I feel happy?*

I had finally achieved my lifelong dream of earning a college degree—something that had once seemed so unattainable. I was now an educated man with a bright future, quite a far cry from the little boy who had to eat garbage to survive. However, that little boy was still inside of me, and that will never change.

The echoes of my harrowing past, combined with the recent loss of Rachel, dug me into a deep pit of depression on a day that should have been marked by the free-spirited sense of accomplishment and release. Instead of feeling self-congratulatory, I was afraid I might collapse under the weight of loneliness and uncertainty. *What am I so afraid of?* I had asked myself during the commencement speech, my mind miles away from the encouraging words of the speaker. I had been alone before. In fact, I had spent most of my life alone, fending for myself. So why was I reduced to tears now at the slightest provocation?

Now that I knew what affection and companionship felt like, it was impossible to turn back. Now that I had experienced the sweet sense of togetherness and felt the warmth of belonging, I could no longer be satisfied alone. When Rachel said good-bye, she had taken with her far more than her physical and emotional presence—she had taken my entire sense of security as well.

As my name was called, I walked across the stage in my cap and gown, feeling nothing but numbness with every footstep. In a blur, I shook the dean's hand with a forced smile. I knew I should feel proud of myself, but the gap in my heart was too big for a single piece of paper to fill.

All at once, hundreds of hats flew into the sky as whoops and cheers filled the air. The new graduates swarmed into the crowd, embracing their parents, siblings, boyfriends, and girlfriends. It was a joyous day as everyone posed for pictures, smiling brightly at the wide open world before them. I waded through the crowd like an outcast, oblivious to the joy around me.

Skip and Becky were there for me to share in my joy, so were Bobby, Caleb, and my oldest foster brother, Chris. I had mixed emotions about this day. While I was happy to have my family there and meet up with my friends, I also felt empty and hollow. The uncertainty of the unknown future loomed before me. I felt as if one battle was over and another one was just beginning.

After graduation, I headed off to summer camp for the last time. It was a nice way to round out my college years before tackling the real world. Camp provided a small respite from my worries, however brief. I still laughed and played with the kids, but I did not feel as carefree as I had in previous years. Whenever I found myself alone, my worried thoughts strayed toward the impending future.

Now that I had a nursing degree, the possibility of going to medical school seemed closer than ever. At night, I fantasized about what I would say in interviews. I knew my grades did not put me at the top of the class, but I thought I could convince a school to take a chance on me like Carroll College did. I had proven myself once; I could do it again.

When I was a homeless child roaming the streets of Manila, I prayed to God to help me make a better life. I promised that in return, I would someday return the favor by helping others. I itched to get started by applying to medical schools, but my self-doubts and my empty bank account crashed me back to reality.

After consulting with Becky and Skip, I decided to work as a nurse for a while and then figure out what to do. There were a lot of opportunities to help people through nursing. Becoming a doctor would just have to wait. I did not regret this decision in any way. I realized that by doing that, I was still fulfilling my need to help others.

My last summer as an assistant nurse at camp flew by more quickly than I would have liked. I almost wished I could freeze time and remain a carefree camp nurse forever. Instead, the trials of adult life were waiting when the summer was over.

My Third Parents—Reno & Becky—with Adriano, me, and Bobby.

Epilogue

I buckled my seat belt, leaned back in my seat, and prepared for the long flight ahead. In seventeen hours, I would step off the plane in the land of my birth for the first time in twenty-three years.

Excitement and trepidation surged through my veins as I wondered what I would find. My body and mind were restless, but emotionally I felt numb. I'd wanted to go back to the Philippines for such a long time, to see the land where I was born and bred, where I had suffered and wept, where I had learned the meaning of hard work and perseverance. I sought the place that I had tried so hard to forget; I was returning so that I could remember. I wished my brothers could go with me. I thought back to the excitement of our very first plane ride when we left the Philippines; we hadn't even known what a plane was back then.

I remembered it well. It was the most painful day of my life. I was not bleeding, my bones were not broken, my skin was not cut, and my face wasn't beaten…but my childhood was stolen. My innocence was tarnished. I was robbed of my trust. Standing outside the orphanage, the painful memories came flooding back. I struggled to compose myself before going inside.

I looked up and down the street, remembering all the times I had lingered on the curb as a child, waiting for parents who never appeared. On either side of me, the large double gates stood wide open, just as they had when I lived there.

When I worked up the courage to step through the orphanage gates, it was like I had stepped back in time. Nothing much had changed. Kids and teenagers loitered unsupervised around the property, some playing games, others standing and talking, a few just staring sadly into space. Some of them glanced semicuriously in my direction as I talked to the guards and explained who I was and why I was there. But for the most part, the kids were too embroiled in their own turmoil to care about a stranger in their midst.

I headed to the reception area, remembering the terror I had felt the first time I walked that path with my little brothers. Mrs. Santacruz was no longer there, but I explained to the receptionist who I was. She told me that most of the house parents from back then had changed jobs or retired, but the facility nurse was still the same. I could not wait to see her again because I had such fond memories of how well she had treated me when I was in her care. As I walked with her toward the tree I had fallen from, I reminded her of how I broke my arm and showed her the scar from the break.

As I toured the orphanage, I was saddened to see that the buildings were still in the same decrepit state that they had been in when I had lived there. Only now, the walls were even dirtier; the peeling paint stained black and brown with smudges of dirt. The rooms seemed even more dingy, with filthy floors, tattered Venetian blinds, and the same hard metal beds upon which my friend, Sonny, had been electrocuted. The bathrooms had not been updated, and there were still no real showers. My heart mourned for the kids who had to live in this squalor.

I longed to reach out and connect to these sad, lonely youths who stared at me with sorrowful eyes as I inspected the orphanage, but I had long forgotten my native Tagalog, and the children did not speak English. When I looked into their eyes, I saw myself at that age; I felt their loneliness and desperation, their fear and anger. I yearned to tell them there was always hope, no matter how bleak their lives seemed. I wanted to beg them not to succumb to violence, thievery, or substance abuse. I knew that their lives were on the edge, and they could fall either way. I also knew what a difference it could make if they felt that someone, even a stranger, cared about them and wanted them to be happy.

My Third Parents

I had an idea. I went back to reception desk and asked if they could organize the kids together so that I could speak to them while someone translated. I explained that I wanted to give them hope and to show them that through patience, faith, and perseverance, it was possible to rise above their poverty and loneliness.

The house parents gathered the kids in the courtyard so that they could listen to their special visitor. I looked around at their faces; most were quiet and solemn, some looked scared and sad, while a few looked bored and defiant. I saw remnants of my past experiences echoed in every emotion I now saw in the kids in front of me. It was almost like looking into a mirror that took me straight back into the past.

Through the translator, I explained to the orphans who I was. I told them that when I was a child, I was just like them. I lived and worked and played and suffered in the same orphanage, staring at the cottage walls, running around barefoot, waiting every day for my parents to come and get me. I talked about my two younger brothers, how we looked out for each other and held each other at night while we cried for our mom and dad.

Tears welled up in the children's eyes as soon as I mentioned how much I had yearned for my parents. I could see in their eyes that during the night they were longing for their mother's touch and their father's protection. Some of them had brothers and sisters to hold them through the lonely nights, but many had to cry alone. As the orphaned children stared at me in silence, I knew that they were feeling what I had felt when I was there. It broke my heart to see that there were still kids having to go through that kind of pain, living out their childhoods in such an unfeeling and lonely place. I was careful with what I said; I did not want to make them sadder than they already were.

After talking to the kids, I watched them disperse. They ran around the orphanage with no supervision and nothing to do. As I looked at the kids, I thought of my two young boys at home; I could not imagine them ever having to be in a situation like the one I grew up in. A lot of kids at the orphanage were my sons' ages. When I looked at their skinny limbs, their scab-covered legs, and their hollow eyes, I saw myself and Adriano and Bobby.

I resolved to help these kids. I knew I could not cure the loneliness the orphaned children felt at night; I could not ease the pain of being a forgotten child. This was something they would have to live through on their own. I could not promise them a better future; I could not stop the violence and abuse. But if they had to be stuck in this awful place, I wanted to make it as bearable as I could. I would do everything in my power to make their time in the orphanage more sanitary, healthy, and safe. I would do whatever was needed to make sure they had shoes on their feet and enough food to eat. I wanted these kids to have the chance to make something of their lives.

Before I left Kabataan for the day, I spoke with the receptionist and house parents about what the orphanage most needed and what I could do to help. Their needs were fairly simple, by American standards: they needed a refrigerator, a washing machine, a rice cooker, and shoes for the kids, among other things.

As I made a list of what I could provide for the orphanage, I remembered the vow I had made when I was ten years old and living on the streets. I had promised God that if He helped get me out of that situation, then I would one day help the other orphaned, abandoned children. Now was the time to start fulfilling that promise.

On my way out, I looked at the guard standing watch by the gate. It was a different guard, but he wore the same impassive expression. This time when I walked out of the gates, the guard did not hold me back.

That night, I could not sleep. I was too worked up from my emotional day, so I left the hotel and looked for the streets I had roamed when I was ten, the streets where I had slept and picked through garbage during the night. As I walked, I saw young boys and girls wandering the streets. Their clothes were dirty, their hair disheveled. Some looked lost and hopeless.

My Third Parents

Others kept their eyes glued to the ground as they moved, looking for anything that could be of use. A few kids tried to sell things, flowers and fruits, to passersby.

It was not long before I reached the shantytowns, crammed with dilapidated clapboard structures pieced together from scavenged bits of wood and rusty corrugated tin. In many places, the tiny slapdash houses were precariously piled one on top of the other, looking like they could fall apart at any minute. Entire families lived in these ramshackle dwellings that were no bigger than my kitchen back in Florida. As I observed the filth and destitution, I realized how truly lucky I was to have been adopted. Things may not have worked out between me and the Mays, but I was grateful to them for bringing me and my brothers over to the United States, where we had a chance to lead fulfilling lives.

As my memories of the streets came flooding back, I visited the bridge where I had showered under the pipes and where I had gotten drunk on gin at age eleven. The scene under the bridge was still the same: drunken teenagers, barefoot street kids, and people sleeping on cardboard. I recognized the familiar smell of the polluted river and remembered the many lonely nights I had spent on top of the bridge, gazing at the stars and wishing for my mom.

I walked late into the night. Jet lag kept me awake; my body had not adjusted. It was not long before the city was asleep, except for a few boys pushing a wooden cart as the moon rose high overhead. I stopped dead in my tracks when I saw them. A chill ran through my body. Without a moment's hesitation, I walked up to their cart and handed them one thousand pesos. The boys were astounded. Because they did not speak English, I could not explain my actions to them, so I simply smiled, shook their hands, and walked away.

The next day, I returned to the orphanage, taking with me a new fridge, a large-capacity rice cooker, and a new washing machine, along with a generous supply of antibiotics for the clinic. I treated the kids to an all-American picnic that afternoon and watched with delight as they eagerly devoured the hot dogs, which they had never tasted before, and washed them down with soda. After lunch, I passed out handfuls of candy to each kid. I remembered Adriano's disdain when the orphans used to trample each other to get the candies that were tossed to them by visiting Americans, so I had them all sit down quietly before I passed out the candy, making sure everyone got an equal amount.

As they chewed on their treats, I squatted next to each child and traced the outline of his or her feet onto pieces of white paper, carefully marking their names next to their footprints. I left the orphanage that day with 150 outlines and returned the next day with 150 pairs of brand-new shoes in exactly the right sizes.

I felt gratified in helping the children at the orphanage. It was rewarding to see their excitement and appreciation, but even though the orphaned children seemed happy, I could see through their smiles. I knew that material goods, while truly appreciated, were not enough to fulfill the emptiness in their hearts.

I had grown up in the same kind of poverty, but I came of age in the land of plenty. I was one of those few individuals who had the rare privilege of experiencing both worlds. Now that I was an educated man with a successful career with a doctoral degree in nursing practice and a master in business administration, I felt it was my duty and my mission to help those who were in need. In a country where 30 percent of the population lives below the poverty line, I wanted to reach out to the most vulnerable sector of that population: the abandoned, neglected, and abused youth who had nowhere else to go and no one to look after them.

I knew exactly how they felt and what they were going through. These children were weakened by fate, rendered helpless by events over which they had no control, and overwrought with feelings of inferiority. They were brutally aware each minute that no one cared for them and no one wanted them. It was a pain that would never be eased, no matter how far they may travel in life. The emotional scars would linger long after the physical scars had healed.

The orphans who wound up at Kabataan were kids who had been abandoned or neglected by their parents, kids who had lived on the streets, kids who had been maltreated or abused in any number of ways—physically, emotionally, and sexually. Without nurturing families for guidance and support, these children developed behavioral and psychosociological problems that could haunt them for the rest of their lives. Without the unconditional love and compassion of a family or parent, the orphans were left with nothing but vulnerability and confusion as they constantly looked for something or someone to fill the unbearable emptiness within. For these kids, life was about survival. The only world they knew was a cold, uncaring one where hostility lurked around every corner, so they did anything they could to survive and not wind up on the receiving end of a punch or a kick.

The orphans at Kabataan were waiting to be adopted, but only some would actually get chosen. Most of them would spend their childhoods in the orphanage or on the streets. I hoped to bring a shred of light into these children's lives because I knew how much of a difference it would make. On the long plane ride back to the United States, I resolved to return to the Philippines as often as my schedule would allow to support the orphanage and help it as much as possible to become a place of safety and support for the kids who needed it the most.

Upon my return to the States, I put the wheels in motion. I founded a charity called Kabataan (Children in Tagalog) Charity, which was granted 501(c)(3) status so we could accept donations that would be fully tax-deductible to the donor. I assembled a board of directors and set up a mission statement:

> The Kabataan (Children) Charity has been established to provide medical and educational support and volunteer assistance to orphanages in the Philippines and children's shelter in the US. We encourage adoption through existing placement agencies. Our primary funding is through philanthropic donations by individuals and corporations.

As the charity began to gain momentum, a fire raged through the orphanage. Several buildings, including some of the cottages, burned to the ground. The children were moved to another orphanage, and the charity continued to help rebuild and improve the orphanage.

The kitchens and bathrooms were modernized to make them more sanitary, and the bathrooms finally included brand-new showers so that the kids could wash themselves without getting scabies. The charity also raised funds to rebuild the clinic. We tore down the old building and expanded the examination room, sick-bay rooms, dental rooms, and physician rooms. I returned to the Philippines regularly to resupply the medical clinic with antibiotics, vaccines and other medical supply as well as educational materials.,

As I gazed at the before and after pictures, I could hardly believe the difference. Now the orphans would benefit from updated, sanitary living conditions and better resources. For children who had nothing, just having the basics was a huge step forward. The children and the house parents drew a huge sign expressing their thanks for the new clinic, their faces beaming at the camera as they stood behind the poster.

Visiting the Philippines always reminded me of how lucky I had been throughout my life. I endured many unspeakable hardships, but I also experienced much beauty and grace. I had learned how to give and receive love and how to place my fate in the hands of Providence to guide me through the unpredictability of life. Despite all my misfortunes and sorrows, at the end of the day I would not change a thing. The events of my life shaped my character and made me who I am. By returning to Kabataan to start the charity, I was able to turn my greatest source of pain into my most valuable strength: my ability to help those who were in need. By helping others, I was healing myself, ensuring that my past struggles were not in vain. Although I could not answer the orphans' unfulfilled prayers, I knew that a gesture of love and compassion might grant them a moment of hope that would make their stay in the orphanage seem shorter and more bearable.

My Third Parents

After everything I had been through in life, I was thankful for what had been given to me. I was thankful for all those people whose paths I crossed who tried to help me, such as the Mays and the Stutleen's my cousins; my high school counselor, Mrs. Ritter; and my third parents, Reno and Rebecca Kuehnel.

About the Author

Fernando Kuehnel is married with three children: Fernando Jr., Tyler, and Andrea. Fernando has a doctorate degree in nursing practice, a master of business administration, and is a registered nurse. He works for a pharmaceutical company as medical science liaison. He continues working to improve the life of orphan children in Manila.